The Light Within:

A Travel Log of India

The Light Within:

A Travel Log of India

⁕

Joseph L. Anderson

PRESS 53
Lewisville, North Carolina

Press 53
6610 Shallowford Road, Suite 202
Lewisville, NC 27023

First Edition

Cover design by Elisa Barger
Cover photography by Joseph L. Anderson

Quotation on pp. 28-29 from *Life of Pi*
© 2001 Yann Martell

www.Press53.com

www.calcuttafund.org

Library of Congress Control Number: 2006935512

This book printed in the United States of America
on acid-free paper

ISBN 0-9772283-9-8

For dad

"Seek to do brave and lovely things that are left undone by the majority of people. Give gifts of love and peace to those whom others pass by."

— Paramhansa Yogananda

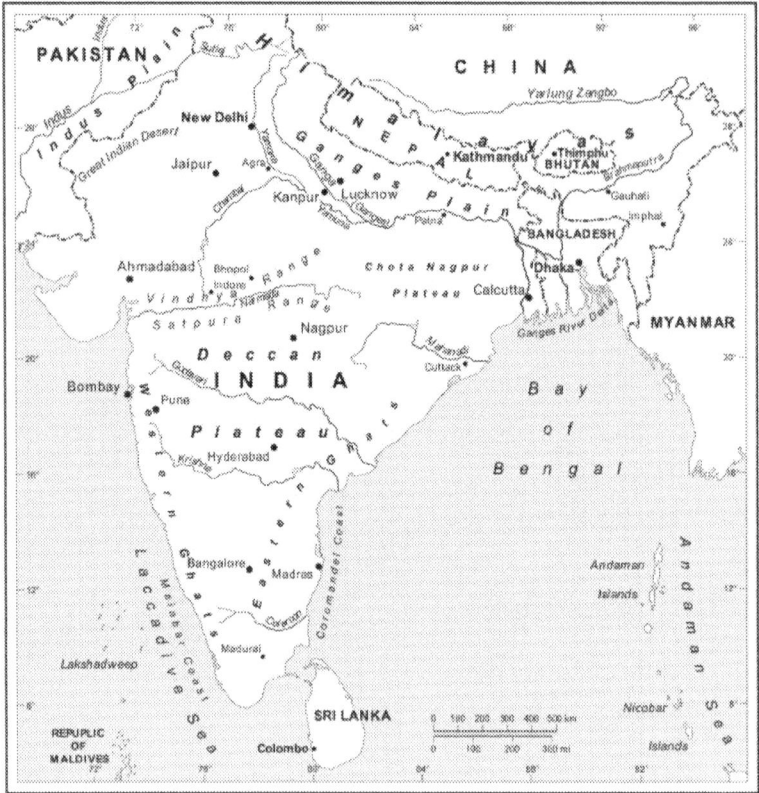

Itinerary

London

Night Crossing	19
December 13, 2004	
Café Nero	21
December 13, 2004	
Sleep Comes	24
December 13, 2004	
Reiki Studio	27
December 13-14, 2004	
British Museum	29
December 14, 2004	
Malaysian Food, etc.	32
December 14, 2004	
Pub Crawl	35
December 14-15, 2004	
Tate Modern	37
December 15, 2004	

Paris

Eurostar	43
December 16, 2004	
Detour	45
December 17-18, 2004	
Passage to Delhi	46
December 18, 2004	

Touchdown 52
December 18, 2004

Dehli

First Night 57
December 18, 2004
On the Loose in Delhi – I 63
December 19, 2004
On the Loose in Delhi – II 73
December 19 - 20, 2004
Vomit and Such 89
December 21, 2004
Of Lotuses, Great Souls
and Dwarves 91
December 22, 2004

Agra

The Road to Agra 99
December 23, 2004
Agra Fort 102
December 24, 2004
A Dream in Marble 108
December 25, 2004
No Matter Where We Are 111
December 26, 2004
Against The Grain of Things 114
December 26, 2004
Tidal Wave 118
December 27, 2004

Jaipur

Roadkill 125
December 28, 2004
"The World Endures But an Hour" 129
December 28, 2004
Pink City, Amber Fort 131
December 29, 2004
Coins, and the Realm 137
December 30, 2004

Calcutta

His Repertoire 145
December 31, 2004
Hear the Bass Drum 149
December 31, 2004
Sighting Everest 151
January 01, 2005
The Origin of a Species 152
January 01, 2005
Clockwork 154
January 01, 2005
Mecca 157
January 01, 2005
Among Gods 163
January 02, 2005

Bangalore

The Way to Bangalore 185
January 2, 2005

Adventures in Silicon   190
    January 3, 2005
The Oberoi Barber   196
    January 3, 2005

Kozhikode

The Poetry of the Moment   201
    January 4, 2005
Music   204
    January 4, 2005
Kozhikode Kamikaze
(or: How I Wound Up in Cochin)   205
    January 4, 2005

Cochin

A Flick of the Brush   215
    January 5, 2005
Vinaya's Song   220
    January 6, 2005
Vyppen   223
    January 7, 2005
Lost   230
    January 8, 2005
The Boatman's Tale   231
    January 8, 2005
Last Day in India   240
    January 9, 2005

Paris

Pre-Dawn in Paris   247
  January 9, 2005
Silvered   252
  January 9, 2005
Paris, Yoga, Louvre   255
  January 10, 2005
Napoleon, Orsay   261
  January 11, 2005
Yoga and My Man Picasso   266
  January 12, 2005
The Thing About My Dad   268
  January 12, 2005
Another Confession   270
  January 12, 2005
Reflection   271
  January 13, 2005
The River Flows   273
  January 13, 2005

London

London, Once More   279
  January 13, 2005
Wormhole   279
  January 14, 2005

Author's Preface

I am a yogi. In 2004, it was my dream to travel to India and practice with one of the living masters of the art, Yogiraj Bikram Choudhury. Near the time set for departure, my father died unexpectedly.

Dad was much more than a parent to me: he was one of my closest friends and a primary role model for my life. The loss of him shook my world. And his death sent my mother, his wife of more than forty years, into a tailspin. It seems strange, looking back, that I proceeded to India during the spasm of our grief. But my mother wanted me to go, not just in spite of our loss, but somehow because of it.

I promised to write. Given the time zones and distances involved, and the vagaries of the Indian telephone and postal services, a web log, or "blog," seemed to provide the most immediate means of staying in touch. I could duck into a cybercafé anywhere and leave an entry she and a few close friends could read when, half a turn of the globe later, they woke up. This little book is that blog.

The death of a man's father calls to mind his own mortality, of course, but also raises searing questions about what is really important in life. *What matters?* I kept wondering; *What should I do before I die?* I walked alone for weeks among the most impoverished souls, wrestling with these questions.

I beheld many horrors. At times I believed in nothing at all. Yet deep within the slums of Calcutta, the street urchins—little children without families, without possessions, seemingly without dreams—reminded me that hope is stronger than despair, and love can conquer fear. In a sea of darkness, there was light within them, a light which, in the end, returned to me.

Joseph Anderson
North Carolina

London

Night Crossing
December 13, 2004

The night was very long. Already exhausted by recent events in preparation for departure, rough skies over the Atlantic kept me out of sleep, and by dawn I was dizzy with fatigue. Additionally, my back, which had been cramping, was now reduced to an inflexible board. Stiff and tired doesn't begin to describe how I felt.

I deplaned and boarded the high-speed Gatwick Express direct to central London, and was instantly immersed within another world. Strange accents abounded, and train announcements were repeated in five languages.

America is so provincial by comparison. True, we are increasingly experiencing interaction with our neighbors to the South, the denizens of Mexico, Central America and beyond. But racist stereotypes, backward immigration policies and the sheer scale of the geography involved make anything approaching the multicultural stew of Europe unthinkable.

The miles chattered away, and as I gazed out the rain-streaked window, I wrote a poem:

Brown thatch rooftops
under somber skies,
and sheep contained by hedgerows;
naked trees, the steeple's peak
behold, the English countryside.

The reality of the voyage began to set in when I walked away from the train. Caught up in the crowd of international business travelers and others on their way somewhere, I caught myself adopting my usual long stride and, truth be told, hurrying along with the rest of them. Then it hit me: there was no point in hurrying. I had absolutely nowhere to go.

I would use Europe as my base camp, spending some time here at both ends of the journey to reduce the effects of the time change to India.

I emerged from the London Underground precisely where I'd imagined, smack in the center of Piccadilly Circus. It was bitterly cold, see-your-breath cold, a shock to the system. I pulled on my only thin gloves and moved north, away from the frozen concrete in search of somewhere warmer.

Café Nero
December 13, 2004

I exchanged some money and have repaired to the Café Nero on Piccadilly Street to think and write this now. I have slept very little of late, but am more energized than tired. It's nearly lunchtime here, though at home it's barely 6:00 a.m. My goal is to stay awake as long as I can, then sleep only until dawn in London, a new time zone, a new day.

Around me in the café people are smoking and talking excitedly over coffee in incalculable tongues; nearest me, four French-speaking Algerians are in some kind of disagreement. I can't say what it is about, but the import of the conversation is clear. Emotions are universal and often conveyed viscerally, regardless of the language.

The gentleman to my right has elected to consume a large, crusty-looking croissant. He is editing a manuscript entitled, "The Odyssey: A New Reading." I would love to strike up a conversation, to know what is new about his reading of one of my very favorite works, but the bespectacled Israeli appears focused and intent, so I leave him alone, exactly the way I wish the One-Eyed Sombrero Man would me back at my favorite café in North Carolina.

The One-Eyed Sombrero Man started coming to the café a month or so ago, and I noticed him immediately. It would have been difficult not to: his sombrero is very large, woven of multi-colored reeds, and never leaves his head. I stole glances at it in bemused surprise, surreptitious because I did not want to provoke a conversation. This went on for about three weeks. Then one day he paused beside my table. The One-Eyed Sombrero Man insisted on talking to me. He hasn't stopped since.

I suspect he is both highly intelligent and mentally ill. His thoughts on life in America are at once insightful and delusional. But the point is, nowadays I have a hard time composing even a single sentence at my favorite café in North Carolina, for every time I start to crystallize a thought in words, he comes to my table. His constant interruptions torment me, and I gnash my teeth as half-formed thoughts escape, sometimes never to return. But I haven't had the heart to tell him so. For all his rambling diatribes, he is amiable enough. I only wish he would leave me alone.

So I won't interrupt the man eating the croissant; I won't learn what is new about his reading of *The Odyssey*. I will spare him that to which I have been subjected. I may not be a One-Eyed Sombrero Man, but the point is just the same.

Sleep Comes
December 13, 2004

At 1:00 p.m. I started getting hungry. After roaming around Soho in the screaming cold for an hour or so, I washed up at a little Indian dive called Bombay House, where I dined on aloo ghobi and garlic nan. It was a good, satisfying meal, and afterwards I felt extremely sleepy. I was so tired, in fact, that my hands shook, and the thought of walking all the way back to the hotel seemed perilous and dark. But I made the distance and collapsed in my room, frozen and exhausted, to the reassuring whir of a thermostat set to 100 degrees.

Not that it mattered. The room, like all of England, remained frigid. The Brits have an uncanny tolerance for cold—and Lord knows they need it. A summer I spent years ago in the English "beach town" of Brighton was the coldest of my life. Being accustomed to frosty, howling weather, Brits pay no mind to such details as caulking around windows and jambs beneath doors. Often there is a windswept crack wide enough to stick a finger through. Even the poshest hotel room in London is liable to be drafty and cold.

Mine tonight is no different: even with all the windows shut and the curtains drawn, an arctic zephyr rakes my bed. And more than that, every time I leave for a while, the maid sees fit to open all the windows, an act so bereft of reason as to give rise to the fantasy that she is secretly conspiring with the One-Eyed Sombrero Man.

The sleep I got, then, was the kind one takes in a shivering lump beneath a pile of blankets so thick as to be almost frightening. I felt that I could smother under there, be lost among the covers mounded up against the cold. I shivered, a kind of autonomic lightbulb producing my own smallish warmth, then abruptly expired into the confusing woods of a terrifyingly deep sleep.

Sometimes, when I am totally exhausted, sleep is like that—scary. My body gives out so completely that I discover myself some hours later face down, arms beneath me and numb, chin smeared with drool. And here's the awful part: even when I do awaken, I am powerless to move. Not merely because my arms are all but paralyzed, their twisted nerves firing angrily, but because I simply lack the will.

And that is indeed frightening. I have become a fetal being, sensate to my own needs but not concerned enough to carry them out. And if I won't look after myself, who will?

Eventually, I did manage to rouse myself, but I wasn't at all sure what time it was. Let me be more specific: I knew from the clock that it was 5:15, but for the life of me, I couldn't tell you whether I had slept three hours or fifteen. Even after peering out my fifth-floor window, I couldn't be sure. If it was 5:15 in the evening, shouldn't there be more traffic? Exasperated, I called the front desk to ask whether it was morning or night. The girl's long pause before answering conveyed without a syllable that, yes, I was an idiot.

Or at least a person very far from home.

Reiki Studio
December 13-14, 2004

After my nap I returned to the streets, vowing to stay awake as long as I could to speed my adjustment to the time change. I wasn't hungry, so I relaxed at The Porcupine, a convivial pub off Leicester Square, taking in the ambience and a few pages of *Life of Pi*. Eventually, I became tired again—it was now about 9:00 p.m.—and made my way back towards the hotel along the crowded streets of Soho, exploring unknown little alleys as I went. It was there that I found the Reiki studio, and stepped inside for a much-needed massage.

Assessing the deformed, bowed contours of my back, the proprietress muttered something in her native tongue and set to work, beating me with her fists and goring me with her elbows for what seemed an interminable time. I cried out and writhed in pain, but for naught; she was bent on saving me.

Forty minutes later I emerged, broken but alive, into the streets of Soho. I had definitely had enough now, and made straight for my room.

Sleep came quickly, the final lamp beside my bed seeming not so much to illuminate the chamber as to steal brightness from it, pulling the light into its massless core. I switched it off.

※

Sleep lasted eleven God-given hours, and when I finally awakened, my back felt better. I was sore at the surface, and literally bruised in places; but deep within me something had started to break loose.

Eleven hours. Never have my circadian rhythms adjusted so quickly to an intercontinental time change. I am up now at 7:30 a.m. writing at the Nero again, and for all I know and feel, it could be dawn back in America. In fact, it's 2:00 a.m. there.

And so a new day—and my trip—begins. I leave you with these thoughts from *Life of Pi*:

"...there will always be animals that seek to escape from zoos. Animals that are kept in unsuitable enclosures are the most obvious example. Every animal has particular habitat needs that must be met. If its enclosure is too sunny or too wet or too empty, if its perch is too high or too exposed—and so many other ifs—then the animal will not be at peace...

"Whatever the reason for wanting to escape... animals that escape go from the known into the unknown..."

British Museum
December 14, 2004

I spent much of today agog in the British Museum. It is a short walk from the hotel, and admission is free. Inside is a feast for the soul.

I have been coming to this place for years; being here again is like a pilgrimage to me. It is among my Meccas, one of my Jerusalems. Within its granite walls lie some of the most perfect and beautiful expressions of the human spirit.

I was captivated once again by that masterwork of homage to the violent end of innocence and beauty, *The Execution of Lady Jane Grey*. The executioner does not flinch, but the viewer does. His victim is so young and fragrant-looking, and so somberly afraid. Her necklace lies useless in the lap of a weeping handmaid; Lady Jane won't be needing it where she's going, and besides, it would be spoiled by the axe's coming blow. The whole world holds its breath in awe of what is about to happen; the painting is a moment of anticipatory horror, frozen in time.

I moved on to the Vermeers, seeing only two, then discovered a wonderful painting by an artist previously unknown to me: it was *The Nativity at Night* by Geertgen tot Sint Jans, depicting an eerie, skeletal angel floating above a darkened scene. I saw works by Bellini, Rubens, Piero della Francesca, Bottecelli, Titian, Raphael, Michaelangelo, Cézanne, Seurat and Monet. I was stunned by *Lake Keitele*, the shimmering, gorgeous image of a winter lake near Helsinki, by Akseli Kallele. But the museum is vast, so I decided to proceed directly to some of my very favorite paintings.

The first of these was Canaletto's *Upper Reaches of the Grand Canal, Venice*. This is a simply impossible work of breathtaking realism; it is all but unimaginable that it was wrought by human hands.

I passed by Renoir's *Boating on the Seine* as though it were little more than a fallen leaf, and treated Cézanne's *Les Grandes Baigneuses* in much the same cursory fashion—though in truth I love both of these paintings. But I was lustily *en route* to the Van Goghs.

Turning a small corner, I beheld it: my favorite painting in the world, *A Wheatfield with Cypresses*, produced during Van Gogh's confinement in the sanitarium at St. Remy, near Arles. I wrote a poem about this painting when I was a child, after seeing it in a book; appraising now first-hand the twisted liquidity of its sky, the fiery energy of its cypress trees, is a dream come true to me. Nearby hung two other masterpieces, also by Van Gogh: *The Sunflowers* and *Long Grass with Butterflies*. The latter also was conceived within the sanitarium and, more than any other work I know, is testament to the strange oneness of madness and genius.

I also saw two Van Goghs that were new to me: *Two Crabs*, an ugly, frightening thing done after the artist had supposedly recovered from his madness and secured release from St. Remy, and *The Zouave*, a portrait making interesting (and for Van Gogh, uncharacteristic) use of primary colors.

Nearby, inside the same salon, and with an irony not lost on me, were the Gauguins. It was a reconciliation in death, one might suppose, for wounds too deep to heal in life.

Malaysian Food, etc.
December 14, 2004

Hunger drew me out of the museum and up the hill, away from the river. Soon I could be found at a small back table in a bustling, steamy little Malaysian restaurant off the high street, ordering vegetarian curry, tofu, roti bread and a glass of sweet, clear liquid bottomed by several pickled lychees. The curry was hot, the bread excellent and the lychee drink bizarre. Chewed at the conclusion of the meal, the lychees were the size and consistency of refrigerated eyeballs: cold, crunchy orbs of sweetness, hollow at their pitless cores.

The waiter and I did not reach an understanding. I ordered, for example, not by speaking, but by pointing at things depicted on the menu. To this he nodded excitedly and smiled, which was in stark contrast to his response when I attempted to order verbally: a fish-like stare. At the end of the meal, I asked him how to say thank you in Malaysian, to which he said something like, "bhruum." I smiled my warmest smile, bowed slightly for added effect and said, "bhruum." Instead of being pleased, he looked at me as though he had just learned I had been living rentless in his basement. I said "bhruum" again, and smiled even more intently, but fared no better; so I slipped away into the drizzled afternoon to hike the streets of London.

All of which brought on a prodigious thirst, so after a while I stopped off at a pub to have a frothy Guinness. It happened to be a Goth pub, heavily spray-painted with graffiti inside and out, its walls lacquered with old handbills for groups like Led Zeppelin, Pantera and Nirvana. A large photograph of a semi-nude woman bathing her breasts in blood adorned the main wall. The hairy pubman poured my Guinness slowly, almost lovingly, then finished his work by deftly carving a pentagram—symbol of the devil—into its foamy head. He handed me the beer with a toothless grin, the stuff of nightmares.

I quaffed it and moved on, strolling away the afternoon in Covent Garden. My long walk took me past the tea shops of Neal Street and the famous section of Central London where all the guitar shops are. I passed the Covent Garden Market and the Lamb and Flag pub, at last returning to the hotel to rest up. I had a long night ahead of me.

Pub Crawl

December 14-15, 2004

The plan was this: I would venture into the dodgy part of town, the Ripper's London—a world of nightclubs, curries and beer. And so by ten o'clock I was standing at the foot of the high stage in a cavernous rock-and-roll bar called Cargo, little more than a converted warehouse, surrounded by the pierced-and-tattooed many. I watched as a three-piece British punk band pounded out a gritty set on trebly Rickenbacker instruments, a living echo of The Jam. Then a band called Guild took the stage and played ballads, Coldplay-style, until hunger overtook me once again.

At 1:00 a.m., I made my way along the seedy backstreets to Brick Lane, that London curry Mecca of curry Meccas. The quantity of food I consumed on this occasion was nothing short of disgraceful. I haven't time to list the many giant, fiery portions, or the infinite variety of spices; it is more efficient simply to report that when my fork rested, the waiter was shaking his head in awe. I did the same when he brought me the bill.

※

It took a long, long time to get home, lost as I was on watery legs within the darkness of Old London, and I was glad to see the hotel again. I slept ten hours and—here's a surprise—awoke to diarrhea.

At dawn, I repaired to the Nero to read the paper and add espresso to the list of recent insults to my innards. Here I learned of new events at Google—the search-engine firm is putting most of the world's great books online—and thanked God again for the miracle of life. What a wonder! How I love the capacity of the Internet to serve as the great leveler, providing equality of access to information unprecedented in the history of humankind. Perhaps as much as the Gutenberg Bible or the advent of the Internet itself, this Google project has the capacity to be a transformational event.

My back is much better today, and I want yoga, but none is to be had. Instead, I will load up my pack, depart for a long walk to the south side of the Thames, and explore the Tate Modern.

Tate Modern
December 15, 2004

I walked the several miles to the Tate. It had become a gorgeous, sunny day, and from the far side of Millennium Bridge I could look back across the Thames and take the view of sunlit St. Paul's, glowing proudly, its dome finally freed from years of scaffolding.

I entered the mammoth Tate, my second visit in as many years. The plan was to start at the top and work my way down, but my senses were assaulted the instant I stepped into Turbin Hall at ground level. Here a "sound work" by Bruce Nauman, which included screams, ghostly moans and a voice repeatedly shouting, "Work! Work! Work!" took hold of my senses; it seemed to mutate eerily, changing dimensions as I progressed through the large, high-ceilinged space.

I can't begin to tell you all I saw and did in the museum, of course, and my report is instead reduced to the inadequate summary of a kind of list, not unlike those pages we skip over in the *Bible* when it goes on and on about who begat whom. But there, surrounded by Picassos, Warhols, Pollocks and Ernsts; there, amid the Miros, Dalis, Rothkos and Magrittes; just down the hall from the lone Rosenquist and around the corner from the lone Modigliani, was August Rodin's masterstroke, *The Kiss.*

I was moved to tears, both by its beauty and its message. The sculpture spoke to me of a subject near my heart of late: the poignant tension between the intense sense of oneness wrought by genuine love, and the impossibility of transcending the fundamental isolation which defines the human condition. Here in Rodin's sculpture, the lovers merge at their mouths. But below, they flow together in a more transcendent way, becoming one united body in the massive marble block from which they were carved. They have achieved the elusive unity all true lovers crave: they are one.

I had been prepared to think about such things by Helen Chadwick's *Eroticism*, an installation piece involving photographic images of two cadavers' brains, side-by-side.

Together, yet apart.

The sun slipped down the face of the sky, and a cold rain gripped London. I made my way across the Thames again to dine within the darkened confines of Gordon's Wine Bar, a crypt-like eatery squatting dankly in a narrow cellar beneath a busy London street.

Candlelight beckoned. I had to crouch to enter the claustrophobic space, and the ancient limestone ceiling freely leached the cold night's rain onto my table, nearly sputtering my candle. But I feasted on baguettes, delicious hunks of cheese and good red wine, taking in the sights and sounds of Londoners. They kissed in corners, argued over business deals, toasted victories.

I crossed the Thames again with shoulder turned against a driving rain, and slept at the Mad Hatter, close to Waterloo station.

Within the giant hold of Waterloo, I knew,

slept the morning Eurostar—my way to Paris and, beyond that, India.

Paris

Eurostar

December 16, 2004

I woke up tired and made my way along Stamford Street to Pret a Manger, where I downed an espresso. Then I submerged into the labyrinth that surrounds Waterloo, navigating its tunnels into the station proper, and boarded the Eurostar bound for Paris.

It was a gray and rainy day, and I was surrounded by noisy, poorly parented children, so I did legal work rather than read or write. I managed to complete and sign my new law partner's employment agreement just as the train emerged from the long, dramatic tunnel that passes beneath the sea between England and France. The import of the document was palpable: by signing, I committed for the first time to sell a major stake in a business I had founded ten years before. It was a *cause célèbre*, the first step in a process designed to free my time spent running the firm. And yet a wistful feeling took hold of me as I signed my name, saying yes to a future I could imagine but not yet see.

An hour hence I reached Paris and emerged from the train at Gard du Nord. Here a smoky little Frenchman tried to seduce me into going somewhere-or-other with him. I declined, instead boarding the Paris Metro and taking the No. 4 line down to the Seine, getting off at Châtelet. There I caught the No. 1 towards La Défense, disembarking at the Palais Royal, the station nearest the Louvre.

I made my way on foot along Rue St. Honoré past the museum, and stopped to write this at La Coupe D'Or (the Golden Cup), a brightly lit café occupied by only the lingering scent of a cigar, its owner vanished.

I'll turn in early tonight; in the morning, I will travel a very long way: to India.

Detour
December 17-18, 2004

I arose before dawn and met the airport bus on Rue Scribe, just behind the Paris Opera House. Away we went in a flurry, hurtling through the darkness towards Charles de Gaulle Airport. I was infused with the excitement of the impending journey, saw myself progressing at last towards the goal. That's when things began to go wrong.

I had started out with plenty of time, but the bus was snarled in traffic, and I began to worry I would miss my flight. Then it happened: the bus broke down. People honked and shouted at us, and the driver ground his starter to an angry nubbin, but there was nothing for it. We were stuck, an island in the river of souls flooding towards de Gaulle.

I won't bore you with the details of all that ensued—the endless waiting, the wan, uncaring faces of the hapless airport functionaries, the standing in long lines only to be told the line I needed was a different line, the petty bureaucrats pummeling my documents with big red stamps, the answer—"*non, non, mais non!*"—the defeated bus ride back into Paris, the sleepless night, the pre-dawn return. Suffice it to say that the next day I was once again whisked away through the sleepy streets of Paris to Charles de Gaulle and, I prayed, beyond.

Passage to Delhi
December 18, 2004

I was deposited at Terminal 2A, Gard du Nord, and leaned against the crowd until I was inside, jostled and jarred by people as diverse as any I have ever seen. They were heading everywhere: these to Teheran, those to Macaroon. Every color, every race of man was represented here. And the beauty was, it all worked. There was no dissent. We were as one body, a tide of beings pouring forth into the world.

They were freighted massively. It was commonplace to see women pushing carts of belongings much larger than themselves, piles of trunks, carpets, baskets and bolts of cloth so towering their owners had to peer out from behind them just to see where they were going. I alone moved quicksilver through the crowd with only a backpack, freed by virtue of all that I did not possess.

There was no retreat from the progress towards embarkation; I was swept along among the packages, the families, the crying children and the staggering old ladies, into the arms of security and beyond. The only escape was by air.

At last I reached my gate and was called for boarding. It took two full hours, though, to load us into the giant hulk of a plane. And no wonder: together we were enough humanity to comprise a small city. I asked a flight attendant and learned that there were three hundred eighty-six of us on board. Of those, I was the sole American.

I adjusted my watch; it was important to set my expectations to Delhi time. Four-point-five additional hours' change. A few quick calculations told me what this meant. At 2:30 p.m.

in Delhi, it would be 4:00 a.m. at home, and so forth.

The radios crackled. The captain's first word: *Namaskar.*

I had finally entered the Indian system.

Without warning, the cabin was sealed and fumigated with dense white gas. People around me coughed uncontrollably, but I held my breath as long as I could. Eventually, I ran out of air and inhaled, sputtering along with the rest of them, my eyes burning.

The aircraft was the largest I have ever seen. Getting it into position was like turning a stadium. We taxied for nearly an hour.

At last the captain lined up with the runway and gunned the engines. They were tremendously loud, but the craft was so heavy that for a long time we did not move. We were sitting on thousands of gallons of jet fuel, sustenance for the long flight. It frightened me to think of it. And yet I knew it mattered not; to paraphrase the Romans, it was a good day to fly.

At last we started to roll. It began slowly but

built like an avalanche until, almost unbelievably, we achieved lift-off. The flaps came up with an horrific metal belch, and we rocketed into the sky. Paris, now suddenly below me, receded quickly. The Seine became so small I could obliterate its image with the tip of my pen. We arced eastward, and away.

We passed Dijon and Neuchâtel, Strasbourg and Berne; there were four thousand miles to go. We passed Basel and snowy Zürich and crossed northern Italy just above Venice, sighting Innsbruck, Salzberg and Linz.

My aislemate, an elderly Indian gentleman who had proclaimed his vegetarianism loudly and repeatedly in the course of insisting that it was past time for lunch, quickly quaffed two largish glasses of wine. By this he was rendered amiable, gregarious, loud.

"Peanuts you have?" he shrieked.

Suddenly an alarm began ringing. For an instant, I thought it was his flight attendant call bell, but it was far too loud for that, and besides, the flight attendants started looking worried.

And it kept ringing.

This went on for fifteen solid minutes. Finally I asked a flight attendant what was wrong.

"We have a problem. I think it is not very bad."

To my left a jumbo jet passed very closely. At last the alarm ceased ringing; no explanation was ever given.

My aislemate abruptly reiterated his dietary preferences; the stewardess was annoyed. She understood, she really did, but sorry Mr. Muthuchidambarum, say what you will, for lunch it is not yet the time.

My food arrived first. I doubt this was an accident of karma; the stewardess was taking her revenge. Mr. Muthuchidambarum was not amused. I begin eating my chutneys, but I could feel his stare hot upon me. I offered him my copy of *Business Week*, but this only seemed to make matters worse; he glared at me and threw up his hands. When his food did come, I don't know which of us was more relieved.

We passed Budapest *en route* to Belgrade, Sofia and beyond, the seatback monitor proclaiming we had reached 35,000 feet. Then

Bucharest, Constantinople and the Black Sea passed by below. Later, Iman. I tried to sleep.

It wasn't easy. Mr. Muthuchidambarum was snoring. It was not so much a snore as a sonic blade that sliced through every other sound on the plane like a crosscut saw, leaving its sonorous edge the only timbre standing. And besides, he had taken his shoes and socks off, and his feet stank.

Notwithstanding these stimuli, eventually fatigue won out. My mind was playing games, making up little songs to go along with the musical mayhem that always fills my head:

> Je m'appelle *Joseph*
> *Anderson I am*
> *swimming like a dolphin*
> *in the skies above Teheran...*

And so forth. I went on amusing myself this way until I became lost within the abstract thicket of a bumpy sleep, my mind an amulet containing only dreams.

Touchdown
December 18, 2004

We crossed in total darkness over northern Iraq, close to Mosul, our ground speed increasing to 600 miles per hour; we overflew Teheran. The Caspian Sea was visible off my side of the plane as an inky nonplace, a black pupil in the eye of the blue world.

My aislemate proved continuously demanding.

"Tea you will bring me?" he abruptly shouted, from what I thought had been a deep sleep.

"Tea!"

The flight attendant scampered away in obedience to his commands.

Turbulence accompanied our mountain crossing at Zaheban and marked our entry into Pakistan. I was slipping in and out of sleep. We climbed to 37,000 feet; coming off the back side of the mountain, our ground speed leapt to 700 mph.

Somewhere in the mountains east of Ispahan we started a northerly turn. Our ground speed now exceeded 760 miles per hour, and all I could see was icy darkness. We had reached the outer limit of my map: we were south of Kandahar, somewhere above the frozen deserts of Afghanistan.

We crossed the Zereh Depression and the Chagai Hills, swooping down across the Central Brahui Range just south of Quetta. Ninety minutes stood between me and Delhi, but we were mired in heavy turbulence, and the huge plane shook so hard and for so long I feared it would come apart. The passengers around me screamed, vomited, and prayed with urgency in unknown tongues, their faces darkly pale.

The Kachii Desert was divided from the Thar by the Indus river; here we found a kind of staggering equilibrium. Now we had only to cross the Great Indian Desert to reach Delhi. My pulse began to quicken with the excitement of a journey near completion, and at the same time, just beginning.

I felt at once intensely alive and extremely alone.

Dehli

First Night

December 18, 2004

The lights of Delhi shone brightly below, and we began a precipitous descent. Although I am an experienced pilot, the angle and rate of the approach left me riveted by fear and drove away the thoughts that had occupied my mind for several days: who would be among the twenty other yogis destined to study with the guru Bikram during the trip? They were from all over the world, and I knew none of them. Would Bikram himself welcome and embrace me as a seeker, or reject me, finding my yoga lacking? Long had I contemplated these questions, but they were of no concern to me now. Trapped within a mammoth bullet hurtling towards the desert floor, my mind adored but one dream: survival.

We landed with a thump at Indira Gandhi International Airport, my ribcage drenched in fear–made sweat. Suddenly the cabin, which had been cool, became breathlessly hot. At once the myriad soporific passengers sprang to life and began the tedious process of disembarkation, freeing unbelievable quantities of every imaginable property from overhead compartments, under seats and even the interstices between armrest and hull. How it all fit is beyond me; the whole affair had the feel of watching someone unzip a suitcase to reveal contents double the bag's original size. There was little room to move; whatever space remained within the fuselage seemed to have been squeezed out toothpaste-style, leaving me straight-jacketed, capable only of shuffling forward inchwise in lockstep unison with the herd.

Eventually, I reached the precipice of the mammoth galley portal, red-eyed, stiff and soaked with sweat. Even so, I was imbued with a relief approaching ecstasy—the end of my long confinement in the aircraft was near.

I stepped off the plane and into another world.

Even the jetway was different. It was filthy, and flies were spinning out the orbits of their lives in it. An odd, feculent odor saturated the air. And posters of svelte bodies contorted into expert yoga postures were peeling from the walls.

I moved hesitantly in the direction of the baggage claim, coming after several minutes of jagged hallways to a mammoth stadium filled from floor to ceiling with acrid white smog. It was so thick I literally could not perceive the baggage carousel, which I later discovered some fifty feet away. Indians loitered here and there as though oblivious to its caustic presence, but I sputtered and coughed uncontrollably, rubbed my burning eyes and struggled to scrape its nasty industrial taste from the surface of my tongue. There was no escaping it.

I waited for my bag, taking in the environs and people around me. The floor was dirty, the walls were dirty and, even after my eyes stopped tearing, the heavily polluted air was hard to see through. And the people: mine was the only arguably Caucasian face within the mammoth chamber. I was among hundreds of descendents of Asia: China, Mongolia, India. Unfathomable dialects increased my sense of isolation.

I found my backpack and began plotting my journey away from the airport and into the city proper.

My research had cautioned me to insist on a pre-paid cab. This was supposed to prevent me from getting ripped off for the fare, or worse. The struggle for my attention among the throng of those who offer such a service was intense, bordering on acrimony, as dozens of dark-eyed taxi agents shouted each other down in an effort to secure my business. I chose a friendly, safe-looking face and committed. He gestured and, without a word, I followed him away.

Soon he was rushing outside the terminal with me struggling to keep up as he nimbly coursed through helter-skelter mazes of men and an all-night construction project the quality of which could only be described as third world. There were few streetlights, and the smog was even denser outside the building. I followed almost blindly.

Suddenly, at a dark and isolated corner a hundred feet beyond the crowd, the sidewalk ended; I stepped off into deep sand, and the man abruptly lunged for my bag. I tried to block him, but he was quick, and he had the element of surprise. Before I knew it my backpack was hanging from his shoulder and he was racing ahead on stubby legs into a shadowy, foreboding parking lot crowded with nearly invisible men, their black shapes merging with larger forms I imagined to be trees and cars. My thoughts were as muddled as my eyesight: was he trying to steal my bag, or enthusiastically leading the way to the car? I wasn't sure. I had no choice but to follow; he was running off with everything I possessed. I knew I could take him if it were only he and I. But would it be?

Things happened next as in a dream. The smog was so stifling I could barely breathe; darkness and smoke enveloped me, confused me. I felt disoriented, and the animal part of me sensed its disadvantage. My jaw tightened. I stood to full height.

An altercation ensued between my driver and some other men. At first I wasn't sure what it was about—they were arguing in Hindi—but was relieved when I deduced the issue was merely which car we could use.

The relief was short-lived. They got louder. My pack hit the ground, the driver's hands now freed for a fight. Shadows moved around me. At once I was acutely aware of my lack of any weapon. I thought of my father. What would he do here? *Wait. And be prepared.*

I took a ballpoint pen from my right pants' pocket, uncapped it, and cupped it in my hand, the point against my wrist. A puncture wound to the throat would surprise, giving me an opening to escape if I were attacked. With my left hand, I reached into the pool of blackness that had to be my backpack, and slung it to my shoulder. The men around me looked surprised at this, but kept arguing.

Eventually, a car was chosen, and without a word, the driver and I piled in and sped away. With a spray of gravel and dust, we hurtled forward into the madness of the main road, into the Delhi night.

It was after 1:00 a.m., but the streets were packed, absolutely packed, with huge, brightly painted trucks. I asked why, not really expecting an answer. In startlingly good English, the driver explained that truckers are only permitted to enter the city at night. They were pouring in by the thousands now, but I was hardly indifferent to their multitude; each truck was a unique, hand-painted work of art bedecked with slogans, colorful sacred imagery and cautionary signs.

At last I reached the Jaypee Vasant Hotel, deeply relieved to be out of the scrum. I was shown to a tiny, dimly lit room, where I threw my pack on the bed with a dusty thud, and settled in for the night.

On the Loose in Delhi – I
December 19, 2004

I awoke to the call of far-away horns, sounding with the arrhythmic randomness of elevator bells, and white-hot light streaming in around the edges of my curtains. It was nearly noon.

The day looked clearer. Over a breakfast of fried beans and toast, I read in the *Hindustan Times* that what I had seen the night before was part of a gigantic inversion layer that had held the pollution near the surface of the Earth, so that the impenetrable foulness that greeted my arrival was, thankfully, unusual.

I later learned that several flights were denied entry into Delhi that night, and twenty-one people died in various kinds of crashes as a result of the smog. I was lucky to have landed at all.

I went to my room briefly after breakfast, but was eager to encounter India on my own terms, and as soon as possible. So immediately I donned shorts, a tank top and my running pack, and headed directly into the streets. I would explore Delhi alone, and on foot.

Nothing in my experience prepared me for what awaited. Within minutes of leaving the hotel I was genuinely shocked, not by the teeming throngs of foreign-looking people, but by the poverty, the filth and the duality of it all:

nearly naked children picked for food atop a garbage heap just yards from the protected enclave of my hotel, literally competing with pigs.

And the *smells*: I was unprepared to deal with them. Feces lay everywhere, absurdly abundant. Piles of it melted in the streets and on the sidewalks. And urinating in public is so commonplace that large puddles of acrid, bitter excrement must frequently be jumped over, gone around or intrepidly crossed.

Dwellings made of plastic, scrap wood and bailing wire were perched atop mounds of rubbish, their wall-rags flapping dustily in a feverous wind. Women bent themselves beneath impossible loads of firewood and water, their eyes sunken. Naked babes plundered haphazardly in the arid soil, their knees calloused, their mouths black with flies.

The squalor was such that I wanted to photograph it, but part of me was deeply ashamed to record the suffering of others using a camera costing more than they would earn in their entire lives.

I walked on, stunned. Sacred cows were everywhere, lounging at the roadsides, on sidewalks, in the middle of streets. Their massive, sighing bodies were obstacles to all; they were things to be got around, or followed for their dung, which men collected and formed into cooking patties with bare hands.

A man passed me with a cage of green parrots, just as two of their free brethren screamed in the hot dry air above. India, a land of powerful and powerless, caged and free.

India asks existential questions, and demands immediate reply. How can you square what you see here with your omnipotent, benevolent God? You can't. What will you make of your life? What purpose do your many pleasures serve when millions suffer unrelenting pain?

As Gandhi said in his "Talisman":

"Recall the face of the poorest and weakest... [Is] the step you contemplate going to be of any use to him[?] Will he gain anything by it?"

Soon matters became more extreme. I had a small map and developed at once an intuitive grasp of the city's organization, essentially a vast ellipsis sprawling outward from a literally medieval core. Still, it was complex. Delhi, after all, is not a single metropolis but an amalgam of eight cities arising here over the course of three thousand years. I was extremely careful with every twist and turn along the way, vowing in my mother's name not to get lost.

Which is what I soon was, though I didn't yet know it. I also didn't realize the path I had chosen for my trek would take me through the poorest, roughest part of the city.

I moved on. People were everywhere—leaning in doorways, squatting at roadsides, lolling atop abandoned carcasses of burned-out cars—and all eyes were focused intently on me.

Women balanced mammoth piles of sticks on their heads, clutched absurdly filthy children almost absentmindedly under their arms. People lay aground, perched in trees, turned food on spits above open flames. Vultures circled overhead. It was medieval, a scene from hell.

Cows meandered everywhere; dogs variously shat, fought and mated in the streets. Chickens were in cages. Chickens puttered about, clucked and ran wildly in the road. Chickens lay featherless on filthy tabletops, their carcasses alive with the kinetic mackinaw of flies.

The stench was otherworldly, a sickly-sweet, curdled mix of excrement and rot. There was no escaping it. The only variation was when its malevolent omnipresence was punctuated by a pocket of something even worse.

Things seemed to happen all at once. Things *did* happen all at once. I was mesmerized by the play of light that shot through fist-sized holes in the outer wall of a temple, light made palpable by the dust that rose from the shoveling required to bury a large dog. As I was watching this, a lime-green parrot began shrieking in the tree above me. Just then a chicken bolted from its cage, tearing helter-skelter through the streets, its erstwhile owner lunging after it. But he was too late, for in that instant an Indian Eagle the size of a wheelbarrow descended like a thunderbolt into the scene, seized the chicken and beheaded it with a single rip of its beak. As I took this in with mouth agape, I tripped over a feral dog suckling six young in the street, oblivious to all around her. In my world, kicking a nursing dog would be cause for horror; in this world, she didn't even notice me.

And that is simply how it went, my first day out in Delhi.

Yet the strangest thing about this realm was the one thing I *couldn't* see: me. I alone was incongruous here; I alone was disconcerting. Every eye stayed trained on me. Imagine the sensation: amid swarms of hundreds, even thousands of people, I was stared at unrelentingly by every person I encountered. It was as though I had descended from the stars.

Naïvely, I hardened my eyes.

I pressed on; by mid-afternoon, I was getting sunburned. Something else was happening, too: I was learning.

I learned, for example, to anticipate what would smell really sickening, as opposed to just awful, and to mouth-breathe through clenched teeth when I encountered such a source (large pools of old urine, fruity garbage heaps, places cows have been kept far too long). Why the clenched teeth? Keeps the flies out of my mouth.

I learned how to smile at the people of India without inviting them to beg, how to decline the overtures of rickshaw wallas in a way that was at once polite and yet absolutely, unmistakably firm.

And I learned to ford haphazard, laneless streets jammed with autos, rickshaws, cattle and dogs without being trampled.

But by far the hardest thing I learned today was how to deal with the begging children.

She approached me somewhere between the heart of the slum and Shanti Path, as gorgeous a child as has ever lived, begging desperately, relentlessly, for any succor I would give. She was about six years old.

Having read in books how alcoholic and abusive parents pimp their children to these streets, and acutely aware that many eyes were watching me, I declined. It's not something I'm proud of, but I ignored her, pretending she was invisible. To do otherwise, I reasoned, would invite a horde.

To this she responded in a manner that was utterly disarming: she fell to her knees and literally kissed my feet. My eyes filled with tears. (They do again now as I write.) I wanted her in my arms, to be one with her humanity, with her filth. But this was a test, and I passed by walking away and giving nothing. The city knew I was not to be taken. The city knew where I stood.

I moved ahead, the pale sun reddening my skin; mile after mile rolled away. Eagles by the dozens carved circles in the smog above. The city smelled foul, but was becoming bearable. I was many miles from the hotel now, and very well aware that I was utterly lost.

It wasn't that there weren't street signs; they were in Hindi script, and I couldn't read them.

Another hour passed, and then another. I kept moving deeper into the heart of the ancient city. Then I reached Shanti Path, and with a huge grin realized I knew just where I was.

It was embassy row, and all were represented here: Sri Lanka, the Netherlands, Sudan, France—so many I didn't try to count them.

I turned right near the Prime Minister's residence at Rashtrapati Bhavan, and there encountered a troupe of large monkeys. They chased me along, clamoring above me on a fence, and seemed eager to bite me—to infect me, I imagined, with an alien bacteriologic stew. When I shook my water bottle at them, they hissed and bared their teeth, but finally scampered away.

I kept walking, mile after mile, hour after hour, until a strange thing happened, and quite by surprise: I fell in love with this place. I love the countless sights, the myriad smells, the animals, the crazy, jarring sounds. I love how life is busting out all over, plants growing up through asphalt, children running free, animals born, nursing, dying before my eyes, the whole cycle of life played out in the anarchy of the streets.

But most of all I love the people, and it is evident that they love me. Once I learned the rules of this place, I began to feel confident I could return a smile without inviting robbery, and the effect was magical. Suddenly, everywhere I went I was a star. It was I, not the cow giving birth five feet from me, that was of interest to the kindly, simple people of Delhi, and when I smiled at them, they seemed to receive more than my greeting: it was as if theirs was an existence somehow vindicated and approved.

The more welcoming I became, the more I was welcomed—a lesson for everyone alive—until at last I was right there with them, foregoing the sidewalks for the inviting entropy of the streets, wondering not how I could remain in India for close to a month, but how I could ever leave her.

On the Loose in Delhi – II
December 19 - 20, 2004

I had worked up a tremendous hunger and, back at the hotel, soon was happily feasting on some of the best Indian food I have ever tasted. It was mostly cauliflower, cooked to an ambrosial crunchiness, and so spicy hot my stomach could hardly take it. But it was delicious.

The meal was served in an opulent hall adorned with storytelling paintings and sculptures of Ganesh. Four musicians knelt on the floor at the head of the chamber, an ensemble consisting of tablas, sitar, percussion and voice. The woman sang, seeming to release from deep within herself a pensive, fragile aura that moved untethered to the framework of the tablas, floating eerily above the sitar's drone like the head of a mesmerized serpent. Hours later, as I lay in darkness in my room and wondered what would happen next, the ancient melody still breathed and turned within me.

I awoke the following morning at 7:00 a.m., my body all but adjusted to the local time. I felt rested and good, ready to resume my exploration of the city. I headed out on foot again, and wound up walking nearly twenty miles.

I made first for Lodi Tomb, a massive sixteenth century temple bordered by a verdant campus of lawns. Incongruously in staid India, lovers lingered here and there amid the shady privacy of giant palms, kissing surreptitiously. I was glad to see it.

I marched on to India Gate, a kind of Arc de Triumph for Delhi erected in memorial to the more than ninety thousand Indian soldiers who gave their lives during World War One; the names of more than thirteen thousand of them are inscribed on the giant arch, and an eternal flame has been burning here since 1971 in honor of the unknown dead. I moved away humbled, proceeding deeper into the city.

And I began to notice something: Delhiites—those few million lucky enough to have a buggy—honk their horns an awful lot. But this doesn't seem to be out of mere annoyance; it's an integral part of how they drive. In fact, most of the little three-wheeled cars have signs on them saying PLEASE HONK. In the madness of the Delhi streets, swirling with pedestrians, animals and runners pulling rickshaws, Indians drive looking only ahead, never behind or to the side. And they don't have mirrors. So they navigate partly by sound, using audible signals to avoid colliding with counter-forces unseen, much the way the blind use Braille to intuit the boundaries of a world invisible.

And I began to decode this complicated language of horns. A single short beep, gently expressed, means, essentially, "Head's up, I'm here." Two short beeps reflect a more insistent determination to be recognized, and contain a dash of urgency, asking, "Don't you see me?" One relatively short yet held-down tone, sort of like a whole note in music, means, "I'm coming into your lane." Two longer tones reflect a modicum of annoyance. And one long, harsh blast means, "I think you are the intellectual equivalent of a squid."

I continued on foot the several miles to Cannaught Place, a mad, circular bazaar of hectic shops of every kind with a radius of more than half a mile. I looked at the hand-carved statues, the colorful saris, all of it—but bought nothing, my purpose instead being to take my first meal *ex hotel.* This was a worrisome but, I felt, necessary task. For how could I fully enjoy the gastronomic delights of India unless my gut had been adapted to the local parasites? Indian cuisine is among my favorites, so this time on the subcontinent afforded an opportunity for culinary adventure that was not to be missed.

My supposed inoculation was accomplished at an establishment called The Embassy, which, according to its legend, had been in business no fewer than one thousand years. This was a claim which might have been true, judging by the condition of its cutlery. Still, it was far and away the best-looking place around, so I dared to eat there, dining on a pungent dopiaza. This seemed—at first—to go well.

At Connaught Place, I discovered merchandising that left my Western mind flummoxed and sent my Western hand scratching my Western head. There were the *petites faux pas,* of course, mannequins missing parts of their heads, things like that. But I'm not talking about those. I passed Cannibal Shoe Store, Thug's Chicken (specializing in home deliveries, no less), and Vitreous Hindware, a maker of toilets. *Hindware?* Yes, Hindware. Wares for the end that is hind. And upon my return to the hotel,

I saw that, yes, this was indeed the very brand of porcelain on which I have been sitting—or, more accurately, above which I have been energetically hovering—these past days.

It goes on. I came to Scam Auto, and then my favorite, The Diplomatic Dentist. My own dentist back in the states is anything but. He is a man who seizes my quivering jowl with whatever grip suits him, peels apart my fright-clenched lips, and stabs me with an unblessed instrument solely of his choosing. Nothing diplomatic about it.

And I saw my first lepers. They were two otherwise lovely girls, walking together in the usual way, but with pieces missing from their hands and faces. The absence of two digits. A section of cheek missing, exposing a margin of jawbone and teeth. The side of a nose, gone, the shadow of cartilage visible within.

And down a narrow flight of stairs that led away beneath the street, I happened upon a young man with dying, gangrenous feet—black, rotting, and stinking from three meters away. My first thought: *they need to come off.* He moaned in obvious pain.

All these things I processed with relative calm. Then it happened: I lost it.

I was in the midst of being accosted by my thousandth taxi driver, begging, urging, nay, *demanding* to transport me somewhere, anywhere, within the sprawling labyrinth of the city. These gentlemen just can't stand to see me on foot, it seems; and they crave my rupees. So they try to corral me any way they can. Most give up eventually, but some are quite persistent.

This one took the prize. He hounded me for ten full minutes, following me, shouting at me, even trying to grab me. Then in a fit of pique he actually rammed me with his taxicab, pinching my body hard between the cab and a solid metal rail which delineated the edge of the street. His dark hand shot out in the direction of my throat. I batted it away, but my legs were pinned. There was nowhere to go.

As if that weren't enough, I had been ignoring a street urchin for a minute or two, and now that I was locked against the rail, struggling with the cabbie, he saw his opportunity. The grimy child lunged for me, quickly filling in my only potential path of escape, and fell upon my pockets with his little fingers. I thrashed, but he was all over me, groping, clawing his way inside…

This was more than I was prepared to take. Surprising even myself, I leapt across the hood of the car, landing in the traffic that surrounds Connaught Place. I had not timed the jump, nor even consciously intended it, so when my feet came to ground, I was dangerously in the scrum, a pod of taxis bearing down on me with horns blaring, and all manner of other moving objects—animals tame and feral, conveyances of every imaginable kind—careening towards me from all sides. I momentarily froze, the urchin still pursuing from behind, then darted straight into the traffic, dodging cars, bicycles, dogs, rickshaws and cows to shake him loose. He didn't dare follow me; I was free.

I decided to leave Connaught Place.

The worst, I presumed, behind me, I would nip up to Delhi University for a look around.

The miles rolled away. Streets were seen, encountered, left behind. The sun beat down, sweat fell, skin glistened. My nostrils burned with the acrid stench of rotting everything. And I came, at last, to a place called Otub Road.

Never in my life will I forget it.

Here a vast river of men and beasts was funneled into an ever-narrowing space which became so tight, so walled on every side, that a kind of Venturi effect took hold, speeding us up to a near run. Sensing the quickening pace, cattle bellowed wildly and hurtled themselves in all directions, threatening to gore nearby pedestrians. Horns blared. Trucks careened. There was real danger of being run down.

Conveyances as old as Hercules looked new against the yokes of oxen, their necks bloodied by the work of pulling half-ton loads. Traffic wove itself like a braid, and I was among the woven. It was medieval, a Bruegel painting come to life.

The edge of the road comprised a manufactory, or rather a series of manufactories, clusters of tradesmen agglomerating organically as though it had somehow been ordained that like kind stay together as one. Here, for instance, were a hundred tinsmen, pounding away at their metals with a clamor to wake the gods; there, just ahead and spanning half a mile of the roadside, were the lumberers, hauling on calloused shoulders the splintered carcasses of giant, rough-hewn beams. All the while the river of men and beasts streamed past, and I was swept along among them.

We flowed into a section bounded by ropemakers, scores of weavers squatting at their work, surrounded by huge wheels of ship-ropes thick as human arms. It was here that a massive Brahman's three-foot horn collided with my ribcage, utterly winding me and leaving a bruise the width of a motorcycle tire. I went to one knee with the pain but sprung up quickly to avoid being trampled by whatever was coming from behind. But I arose to find myself enmeshed in an angry clot of traffic that was grinding to a halt, and I was suddenly trapped between two trucks, one large and blue to my right, the other to my left and smaller, white. My world comprised the narrowing space between them.

We were atop mire. Let me say it simply: I was running on shit. It was terribly slippery. Somehow my backpack became snagged on one of the blue truck's rope hooks, and I was nearly dragged from my feet. But going down was not an option. Behind me was a furious team of oxen driven onward by a wide-eyed, sadistic-looking child. You could tell he liked the crack of his whip. I did the only thing I *could* do: grabbed the lip of the truck and lifted my feet from the ground, hanging on for dear life. At the same time, I fought to protect my legs from the elliptical turning of the truck's gnarled rear wheel. I heard the wrench of metal bending. Suddenly, the clot of traffic broke and the truck burst free, rattling ahead with surprising speed and me still flailing from its steely flank. I managed to disengage my pack strap with one hand, dropped off the truck bed and ran from the street into an alley, hands on my knees, lungs screaming for air.

But I was made. Six small children, filthy and wan, surrounded me; they were trying to pick my pockets. For a moment I tried to be civil, smiling and gently telling them no, but almost instantly all sixty little fingers were wriggling energetically around my midsection. It was like being frisked by an amphetamized sea anemone. I turned and burst once more into the madness of Otub Road, running full steam to dodge the cars, trucks, rickshaws, cows and dogs there, and shook the little band of urchins loose. But now I was back in the river of men and beasts, swept along inexorably towards an unknown fate.

Vultures, now more than ever, circled above. Soon I knew why: we were approaching a large dump. Even from far away, the stench was killing. Acrid, bitter molecules thickened the air, but in the distance I could make out a wall of mangled trucks arising from a field of detritus to a height of several stories. Beyond, and taller still, a giant dune of garbage heaved up like a mountaintop.

Drawing nearer, I beheld the fetid ecosystem of this Martian landscape. Atop the dune, mostly naked children fought with wild dogs and even one another for the meagerest, most fetid morsels: a gnawed husk of corn, a rotting rind of melon, a crystalline trace of syrup in the seam of a discarded plastic bag. Small compost fires smoldered here and there, touched off by chemical reactions deep within the mounds of heterogeneous decomposition. The sky above was black with insects, predatory eagles, and soot.

I walked on and on and on. Eventually I turned right with the mammalian swarm and reached Kashmiri Gate. There I was able to break from the crowd and take to a partially constructed sidewalk. A little farther on, I skirted past some angry-looking monkeys and descended into the subway. By this small act, I made history, for, as it happened, I was one of the first people in the world ever to ride the Delhi Underground.

Prime Minister Singh (for whose intellect, let the record show, I have nothing but respect) declared the subway fit for travel yesterday, and today it opened. But common Delhi had not yet discovered the modern wonder slithering about beneath its streets, so, merely by showing up, I was one of the first to ride.

It was all so quaint. The train was shiny and new, impressively so; but it traveled only a mile, and in that span made but four stops. Only two of these were at any place of consequence. At each station, the doors whisked open and a British voice intoned: "Mind the gap." It was so civilized, a Little London. What a perfectly peculiar thing to find amid the madness of Delhi.

At last, I made it to the university. There I struck up a conversation with Hari, a lanky and startlingly tall Indian youth who turned out to be a computer student. He was wickedly thin; the bones of his shoulders were visible through a threadbare white shirt so old it looked as though it might have been my grandfather's. Eagerly, he volunteered to be my guide.

A patient man, and kindly, he freely gave his afternoon to show me the campus. This included the law library. I was aghast at the abundant moldiness of its contents; undeterred, loyal students hunched across the ancient books, damaging their eyes on fine print smeared with fungus stains.

During the long walk home, I began to reflect on all I had seen. Amid the grinding entropy of the Indian landscape, I realized, the compassion of the Indians themselves shone like a beacon. I thought of Hari, his kindness. Then I witnessed an act of Indian altruism I will probably never forget.

Recall that much of the commerce in Delhi is by foot. Hand-drawn carts are laden with fuel, water, grain, engines, wood. You name it, men are pushing and pulling and dragging it around the city. I was walking along behind just such a cart, dragged by a man so emaciated he deserved the cover of *National Geographic*, when several boxes of goods fell from his carriage. It was then that another man, crippled, lying in mire and even poorer than the first, heaved himself skyward, hobbled on a clubfoot to the dropped goods, picked them up, and *placed them back on the cart*. This he did carefully, quietly, and without the other man even noticing the kindness. Listen to me: he definitely could have used whatever value could be eked from those goods at the local black market. But he didn't steal them. He put them back, and without a word. That, my friends, is how most Indians are.

And they are godly. Shrines are everywhere, and calls to prayer are answered without fail. Any space big enough to hold a marigold is big enough to give to God. In my first days here, I have seen thousands of colorful shrines. They are ubiquitous, popping up in taxis, bathrooms, rickshaws—even the palm of a beggar's hand.

And Indians are artistic. Things taken for granted in America become the objects of great devotion here. Ride from the airport into Delhi, taking notice only of the colorful trucks; you'll see what I mean.

At the end of my long day, I washed up at Vasant Vihar and told the barman where I'd been. He gave me a puzzled look. I showed him the map, and pointed to Otub Road to be sure I was being perfectly clear. He studied it gravely, shaking his head.

"We never go there. *Never.*"

Somehow, that satisfied me.

As I lay in bed writing this now by the light of a small candle, I notice my stomach beginning to rumble. And truth be told, I've had diarrhea all day. Now admit it: there are many things—many—that could be causing these symptoms. It could just be fatigue, brought on by the discombobulation of the mammoth time change. Right?

The other yogis arrive tomorrow; I want to be in top shape to greet them.

It needn't be "Delhi-belly"—does it?

Vomit and Such
December 21, 2004

I have been very ill. In fact, several hours ago I was so weak I literally could not stand. Crawling around on the floor in a hotel in Delhi is not my idea of a good time, but that was the best I could do. To stand was to be extremely dizzy; I risked falling down. So I crawled.

It was 4:00 a.m. or so when the feeling hit me: wrenching abdominal cramps and bloating more insidious than any I have ever experienced. I was full of gas, simply *full* of it; it seemed my abdomen would literally burst. I was put in mind of those sacks the hero used to trap the four winds in *The Odyssey*; I felt as huge and taut as one of them.

I shat and vomited for three straight hours, until I had nothing more to give. Yet still I bloated. I was miserable: my belly throbbed, I was so feverish I became confused, and my intestines wretched and twisted. I went for the Imodium (thank you, Mom) and it really helped. At last I conceded to the exhortations of a fitful sleep.

I had hoped to handle the situation on my own. For most of a day, I did just that, much to my own detriment. But there was nothing for it. Fifteen hours into my ordeal, I was visited by the house doctor, a dignified, elderly man who made house calls and required pre-payment, in cash, on the spot. A tattered business card proclaimed him to be Dr. C.M. Bajaj, M.B.B.S.

He looked me over briefly and declared a bacterial infection of the intestines. Because I was still so nauseous, he injected me in the left buttock with intramuscular phenergan before administering electrolytes, a blue pill he said would help with the abdominal cramping and a strict diet of nothing but yogurt and rice. And, of course, the needed antibiotic. I felt better just being under his care. He was, if nothing else, an ambassador of hope.

He departed, and instantly the noise began.

It was beautiful noise—the ecstatic singing and drumming of a large Indian wedding just beneath my window—but noise nonetheless. It went on unabated, keeping me from any rest, for seven hours. I tossed. I covered my head with pillows. I stuffed things in my ears. I railed against the celebrated union with The Curse of Western Impatience. All for naught.

When at last the pandemonium abated, I almost could not believe it. The silence was that beautiful. I dove into it like a fish returning to the safety of the deep, and slept for eighteen solid hours, dreaming of nothing at all.

Of Lotuses, Great Souls and Dwarves
December 22, 2004

I awoke a new man. I am so happy to feel a little better today that I nearly danced from my room. I had slept, off and on, for thirty hours, and in that span had never once departed my own chamber.

My level of circumspection, shall we say, has

been advanced considerably, and I will be eating only yogurt and bread and taking it quite easy today. I intend to act like a normal tourist, sticking close to the hotel and taking taxis to various monuments and sites around town. And why not? I've already immersed myself in the most exotic aspects of this city. And although I have been paying dearly for my exploratory tendencies, I would not give back the experiences of the last two days for anything, even to spare myself this sickness. (Had you asked me that at 5:00 a.m. yesterday, though, my answer might well have been different.) Anyway, I had overslept and missed the bus that took off into town with all the yogis, so I hired a proper taxi and had him drive me around—like a proper tourist.

I made first for the Bahai house of worship on the southeast side of town. Shaped like a giant lotus flower, it is an architectural feat of genius. Its unbuttressed, spherical masonry ceiling arches to a height of seventy feet, creating an unparalleled reverberation chamber in which the sound of bare feet calls to mind the anthropomorphic whisperings of an ocean rain.

One is required to remove one's shoes to enter the temple; within, one is directed to sit in silence for a time before moving about. As a consequence of these rules, and the sheer magnificence of the structure, an air of real reverence pervades the place.

A brief prayer was held. A man arose and said in English: "Do not seek wealth, or you will destroy yourself as though you were your own enemy," his words lilting skyward in the echo chamber. Then another man sang. His voice was otherworldly, rising like a flood of souls to shimmer in the temple's vast, high-ceilinged orb. It was the sound a mirage would make, melting at the far horizon—if a mirage could make a sound.

My next stop was Raj Ghat. Perched atop the western bank of the Yamuna River, it is the tomb of Mahatma ("great soul") Ghandi, of whom Einstein wrote: "Generations to come will scarce believe that such a one as this ever in flesh and blood walked upon the Earth."

An eternal flame consecrates the tomb; a

verdant maze of gardens surrounds it. I walked shoeless and in silence, pondering Gandhi's legacy, and wondering what would be my own. Enshrined within this tomb was a man whose will to justice had transcended all the corporeal derelictions of the mad world. What would I make of *my* life?

Inhabited by these thoughts, I plied westward to the Lakshmi Narayan temple, an ornate house of worship in the very heart of bustling New Delhi. But my getting across the street and into the temple was confounded by an antagonistic dwarf, who insisted I buy a "sexy" Krishna drawing. (There was nothing sexy about it, and I did not.) He flanked me like a crab, back and forth, forth and back. At last I got around him by literally running so fast he couldn't keep up. Two points to the little bugger for persistence.

Once past the temple's entrance and with feet again manditorily bare, I made my way into an astonishingly beautiful shrine in which, most unfortunately, no photographs were permitted. I was searched at the door and stripped of my camera, a disconcerting step but one that had to be taken: the place was so bewitching no mere promise could ever have prevented me from photographing it.

To enter here was to strip off five thousand years and rejoin a twilight time in which rationality had not yet elbowed aside primeval, childlike idolatry for the great enigma of existence. Here was the ancestral home of the gods, the domicile of Lord Vishnu, the very seat of mystery.

Colorful idols adorned the maze of halls. When at last I reached the inner sanctum, I crept into a shadowy circular room where, surrounded by an orbit of rose petals, a priest was crying prayer in a voice that never rose above a whisper. A half moon of the faithful gathered at his gnarled feet, incense coiling in the air above them.

I crossed the street and ran around the crab-like midget once again, then headed back to the hotel. Although the day was relatively young, the illness had weakened me, and I was already tired.

I decided to retreat into the static world of a

book. It was time for me to learn more about Gandhi, and I found an English copy of his autobiography at a nearby bookstore for three dollars. Then I retired to my room to read and rest, knowing that Dr. Bajaj would be proud.

Agra

The Road to Agra
December 23, 2004

It was a fitful night, the anticipation of joining the other yogis for the journey to Agra boiling within me. For the first time, I would be well enough to interact with the others—expert yogis from all over the world, most of them gurus in their own right.

A pair of large busses would provide passage from Delhi to Agra, site of the Taj Mahal. There, I hoped, we would practice with the master, Bikram himself, several times the yoga champion of all of India.

At dawn we loaded into a bus bound for Munrika, Der Serai and the National Highway south towards Agra. We were following the course of the Yamuna River.

At the outskirts of Delhi, near Govindpuri, we had to pay a toll. No sooner had our wheels stopped turning than the bus was swamped by a mob of the most destitute, medieval-looking beggars I had ever seen. Among them were snake charmers, toothless old ladies and dozens of emaciated children. Faces peered out from behind centuries, then recessed into the pulsing swarm; it was the metamorphic face of all mankind. And though we sat up high in our bus-thrones, voyeurs to their squalor, I felt that morally we were beneath them. When our tax was paid, I knew, we would depart their afflicted world, bound ultimately for Paris, Chicago, L.A. But they would remain here forever.

The road to Agra, like all of India, is bumpy and chaotic. We passed broad swamps of acrid white matter, heaps of cow dung mounded into piles ten feet tall, scores of animal carcasses. There were burned-out cars, women carrying impossible loads along desolate roadsides, myriad animals feral and domestic: goats, cows, camels, monkeys, chickens, sheep, asses. A huge swarm of parrots harassed an eagle. Wild boars rooted atop garbage heaps and sloshed around in roadside swamps. Shantytowns poked out of the shadows of eucalyptus groves, and saffron fields opened all but endlessly to the farthest horizons. Here and there an ancient ruin was melting into the Earth.

We came, near Kosi Kalan, to another scene from hell. Here a scrawny man had a large bear by a leash. Or, more accurately, he had the bear by a chain through a hole he had drilled in the septum of its nose. This struck me as an extraordinarily cruel means of keeping the animal under control. When he jerked the chain, as he did often, the bear contorted in pain, snarled, and tried to bite him. Then the man would beat the creature about the neck and shoulders with a heavy stick. The whole affair sickened me.

So, like a good tourist, I photographed it.

As we moved away from the city and into the countryside, the poverty deepened. And when at last we drew into the outskirts of Agra, my breath was stolen from me. The poverty and compression seemed to multiply together exponentially: the poorer people became, the more cramped their quarters. At last the giant slum was little more than a writhing mass of human larvae, purulent rivers etching random sinus tracts among them, the only organizing force. Here we had dog shit and man shit and cow shit intermingled; there a dead man lay deflated like a spent balloon, receding almost before my eyes into the brown everyman of the Earth, the vast horde simply stepping over or around him and going on its mortal way.

A bus turned over. Trees in flames. Streets of black mire deep enough to pull a shoe off— assuming you had a shoe. An all-but-naked boy chasing a pig up the road with a pointed stick, the goal to kill it with his bare hands, a fantasy in blood. Would these were only dreams.

Agra Fort
December 24, 2004

I awoke within the walled enclave of the Jaypee Palace Agra a changed man. I sensed intuitively yet unequivocally that the time was now to plot a new phase of my life, turning away from an emphasis on self-empowerment through labor and money and towards a more dedicated phase of learning—about the world, others, myself, love, what is called God, and the nature of creativity.

I was inside a shamefully luxurious five-star hotel, at once near and yet light-years away from the human suffering mounded just outside its walls. We had entered through an iron gate, were wreathed in flowers by obsequious attendants, and promptly feasted. Then we showered under conditions which would amaze—and possibly frighten—the common Indian: the subdued ferocity, the angry steam of a good, hot shower, the kind we take for granted. And we slept in beds so clean and white they seemed but heavenly illusions in the black tar universe of the mire that surrounded us.

Within, it is a little paradise, really; behind high walls, we walk on ancient marble floors and fend off rhesus monkeys occupying the verdant moat between the perimeter and our patio doors, ever trying to break in. Signs proclaim: "MONKEY MENACE. PLEASE KEEP YOUR DOORS DOUBLE-LOCKED." And believe me, they mean it. These are monkeys smart enough to open doors, and even single-locking will not do. One mistake and the little devils are in your room, disemboweling the contents of down pillows the way you and I would empty out a laundry bag, eating marigolds, jumping on beds and generally having the time of their lives.

Today we finally practiced yoga. Bikram taught; he very gently killed us. I could describe it as loving us to death.

It was hot. Actually, to say that it was hot is to engage in understatement going well beyond the merely British and swerving into outright misrepresentation. Bikram said it was 110 degrees.

How was this achieved? By moving fifteen propane heaters, the kind they burn on patios, into the sanctity of the yoga room. Part of the preparation seen to by Bikram was to have these brought in, lit, and burning before we even began to practice—not just for a couple of hours, but *all night.*

Bikram was the progenitor of "hot yoga," and requires every studio using his name to conduct its classes at 105 degrees.

In this case, he burned the oxygen out of the room. During the standing series, it was nearly impossible to stand; I was extremely dizzy. I looked down. I saw feet and, below them, floor. This pleased me. But the ground looked slanted and seemed to be shifting around, a pediment designed by demons. The mirror of my mind was going dark.

Still, it was marvelously primal to practice yoga surrounded by a ring of naked flames. Sweat poured off me, and final *shivasana* was a God-inspired dream. With eyes closed, I saw a Viking ship, the sun dying behind it, astride a pointillistic sea. Then I melted.

We ate and headed out to Agra Fort, a red stone structure so massive it defies categorization. If the pyramids were a universe, the Fort would be a galaxy. A hundred Eiffel towers could lie within its barricades with room left over to accommodate the Golden Gate Bridge.

It is a double-walled, deeply moated city-state, the inner fortification rising nearly seventy feet above the desert floor. Begun in 1565 A.D., it was the stronghold of the Mughal Empire—Mughal being the Persian word for Mongol—a Muslim dynasty whose kings were the linear descendents of Genghis Kahn.

We entered by crossing a narrow drawbridge. With the drawbridge up, the Fort would be all but impregnable; I imagine the Mughal warlords loved the sense of invulnerability it inspired. Inside, vast tableaux unrolled within a hidden microcosm: intricate temples, broad fields, wind-torn trees. Whole lives were no doubt lived from birth to death within the walls.

Stories about Agra Fort abound, and the interesting thing is, they are true. For example, one early king, apparently interested in equality of access to justice, set up a chain with bells on it leading from a place near his lofty chamber in the Fort all the way down to the desert floor near the edge of the Yamuna River. The idea was that anyone aggrieved, no matter what his caste, could pull on it, ring the bells above, and appeal directly to the king for succor. Now, the Yamuna is a fluid thing, and its proximity to Agra Fort has shifted over time; but even making the most conservative assumptions, the length of this chain would have to have been at least a thousand feet. And this, fantastic as it may seem, is no mere myth; visitors to the Fort during that period described the chain in their writings, and it is even depicted in one painting from the time.

But no story surrounding Agra Fort is better known, or more emotionally fraught, than the tale of another Mughal emperor, Shah Jahan, whose brainchild was the Taj Mahal.

After being deposed by his own son, Jahan was banished from the Taj to Agra Fort for seven years, and died there. The Fort is so massive that, even compared to the Taj, it is a giant; from its heights, the Taj is clearly visible in the distance with the naked eye. Thus it was that Shah Jahan, creator of the Taj Mahal, spent his last days confined beyond its reach but well within its sight, the Fort ironically transformed from a protective shield into the cruelest prison. It was a fate more tantalizing than anything that befell Tantalus, and when I took the view from Jahan's prison cell, gazing across the open plain separating Taj from Fort, I felt the whisper of a breeze, saw three eagles turning in the azure sky, and felt sorry for him.

The Taj, after all, is so beautiful from here. And unlike Jahan, who is dead forever, I will go there tomorrow.

A Dream in Marble
December 25, 2004

On Christmas Day, I awoke to a misty morn and enjoyed some time alone in my room, reading and writing. This has become something of a ritual with me: I like to write for a while shortly after I arise, while my mind is fresh, my thoughts still uncluttered by the pace of the day. For be it fever-pitched or slow, sublime or beautiful, the colors of the day inhabit us, infuse our being.

We hit another brutal yoga, ringed again by

open flames, then showered, lunched and moved out—this time for the Taj Mahal.

Let me just say it: the Taj is gorgeous. I can't tell you what it is—which line, what curve, what feat of symmetry—but this is a special place. It is indeed so lovely that even as you walk right up to it, you simply can't believe that it is real. You have the feeling that a breeze will surely come, rippling the projected image before you, showing it has all been a fraud. For the first time in my life, I had the sensation of literally not being able to believe my eyes.

Where does the magic lie? It's not the dome, the inlaid lapis lazuli, the Arabic script or even the reflecting pool; it's not the minarets or the clear view of the river. It is the *whole* of it, massive yet lithe, a noble face if ever there was one, eight facets to the ever-changing sun. A dream in marble. The most beautiful building in the world—and all a monument to love.

For the Taj Mahal is the keeping of a promise. Shah Jahan's wife, Mumtaz Mahal, bled to death giving birth to their fourteenth child. As she lay dying, Jahan swore to her that he would build a monument to their love. And when it was completed, he placed her sarcophagus in the center of its main chamber. For many years thereafter, he went shoeless to her grave.

Until, that is, one of those very same children—Jahan's power-hungry son Aurangzeb, who later beheaded his own brother and ruled the Mughals under the nomen "World-Shaker"—imprisoned him in Agra Fort for the rest of his life. When I read the details of Jahan's relentless visits to his dead wife's grave, I was brought to the full horror of his banishment to a place within its sight but just beyond its reach: it was a constant echo of the separation wrought by Mumtaz's death.

Incredibly, we practiced yoga *in* the Taj. We were passing through the Eastern enclave when it happened: abruptly Bikram pulled off his sweats and assembled our band of yogis into three lines, leading us through the practice wearing only a red Speedo. A crowd imme-diately gathered, and by the time we rested, we were encircled by a mob of onlookers and media men, flashbulbs popping and television cameras rolling.

For six more hours I wandered the grounds of the Taj and reveled in its beauty, never becoming bored. The sun slowly royaled to gold, then orange, then crimson; as the stars poked out from the depths of space, it seemed my fate aligned: it was the Taj Mahal, at the height of a glorious sunset, on Christmas Day.

The feeling was difficult to explain, but it had to do with being complete, at home in a universe that contained everything I would ever need, all that could ever *be* needed—even peace.

No Matter Where We Are
December 26, 2004

No matter where we are, no matter what our circumstances, we are alone. A billion neighbors does not change this fact. And, within the walls of the world, within the boundaries of human capability, we are free.

Like so many aspects of experience, this is both affirming and frightening. For we are responsible to be our own creators, the sculptors of this piece of clay we call a life. Freedom is both opportunity and obligation; in the end, it is both a wall of the world, and a doorway we must walk through. Ours is freedom wrapped inside determinism, freedom in chains.

I'm starting to see that the walls of the world—death, aging, mind, physics, existential loneliness (a non-exhaustive list)—are like the crust of a creme pastry within which something soft and delicious can and does exist. Ours is an *interstitial* way of life, life within the moat of certain death, youth played out before the onset of old age, a mind good enough to pit against the problems of our time and yet inadequate, fundamentally inadequate, to grapple with the questions of its own being—a mind, in short, capable of formulating problems it cannot solve. Ours is an existence of arms and legs, all the gorgeousness of a carefree walk on a spring day, but we will never leap into flight, an experience we all relive in our dreams. And our existential loneliness cannot be breached by hands held, lips kissed, eyes gazed into. Here is a bridge that only intercourse of mind can cross.

And yet, within the bony exoskeleton of our little corner of it all, within the steely embrace of old age, death, and the eggshell fallibility of mind—within these walls abides life: long walks on spring days, hands held, lips kissed, eyes gazed into. Words expressed or left unsaid. Lovers chosen or rejected. Decisions taken or put off. This is the soft, sweet stuff of life as it is ours, the creme within the pastry. Here, inside the tortoise-shell of all our limitations, we are free.

So actually, both freewill and determinism are real. One lives inside the other like a Russian doll. The human way of being could no more exist outside the walls of the world than could a baby gestate in the emptiness of outer space. Within our walls, upon the little stage of our experience, what we do is important, if in no other sense than to us. We cannot solve the riddles of our world, and we must surely die; but we can truly love, can hear a child laugh, and take the color of a flower, electrical in its intensity, into our eyes. We can dip our toes in cool springs on hot days, use our minds to do what we are able. Perhaps the hardest task, and yet a thing that also lies within our power, is letting this be enough.

Against The Grain of Things
December 26, 2004

The day was long. We practiced yoga intensely, and after a quick lunch I departed on foot alone into the wilds of Agra. Everyone else was going shopping by bus, but I craved adventure. I simply could not join them.

I headed west, against the grain of things, and managed through a little sandstorm, suddenly finding myself ludicrously filthy. Yet I was undeterred, even exhilarated. Turning south, I wandered into a neighborhood and promptly got lost.

I was looking for an Internet café to write this entry, but what I found were kids—dozens of them. They were fascinated by the tall, blue-eyed foreigner. I felt like the pied piper with my little train of thirty young admirers running after me.

At last I found a dingy cyberpoint, little more than a mud-walled box of dead air squatting dankly in a half-lit basement. But I was thrilled to see that there, beneath an orbit of boisterous flies, was indeed the object of my mission: a computer.

Sort of. The machine was ancient, looked as if it had been whipped with a muddy rope, and ran a pirated, bug-ridden version of Windows 95. It also lacked the software driver I needed to upload pictures from my substantially more modern camera. But a dark-eyed boy named Abdul Quadin gladly spent two hours working with me to download the needed driver from an Indian website. The effort required for this project was far greater than could have been imagined, and our struggle provided the afternoon's entertainment for a small crowd of bearded old men in Coke-bottle glasses, flowing robes and bone-white turbans. They gathered behind us, peering over our shoulders to point curiously at the computer and whisper things in Hindi—presumably about our lack of progress. At last the camera booted, and a small applause erupted from the wrinkled little crowd.

The afternoon died, and the hot white light of day turned yellow, streaking the concrete staircase leading to the basement's doorway in a deepening glow. Outside, the air was filled with the din of the call to evening prayer, an exhortation broadcast from the rooftops via ragged speakers propped atop rickety spires, each connected by an umbilicus of wire converging in an invisible, homespun web whose ultimate terminus was, I supposed, a microphone clasped by a wizened, veiny hand.

The stairs turned blood red, purple, then gray, and I departed, making my way home through a tangle of dusty, moonlit streets. Here and there men poured water on themselves from battered pails, the commoner's bath, and the colorful smells of unfamiliar foodstuffs filled the air. The final hint of sunlight gone, the streets went pale in the milky luminance of the moon.

I came to a place where a man was beating a chained horse mercilessly, hitting it hard across the face with a log as thick as a bat. The animal screamed, and I felt the pangs of its terror. I wanted to intervene, but didn't dare confront a man both armed with a heavy cudgel and so obviously prone to use it. And besides, in this realm, the horror of his violence was little more than an especially fulgent ripple on the sea of pain in which the world was drowning anyway. Better to simply move on—and remember.

Back at the hotel, I washed the street's filth from my body and went down to dinner. Bikram had arranged another sumptuous banquet, this time with a Mughal theme.

The food was served, appropriately enough, inside the giant chamber that had been our yoga room. We dined in opulence that couldn't have contrasted more distinctly with the poverty of the slums in which I had spent the day; our dinner chamber seemed the lair of Aurangzeb himself.

We sprawled on mounds of pillows and were entertained by Mughal dervish dancers, traditional tabla drumming and the throaty sermon of an ancient sitar, dark as ironwood and scarred by the indifferent hands of time. When at last I retired to my room to read, think and sleep, I turned the final page of *Life of Pi*, wept for the nobility of its premise, and clicked off the light.

Tidal Wave
December 27, 2004

Now begins the fifteenth day of my wandering. Imperceptibly, time has been slipping by; it is time again to clip my fingernails. I find myself awake at dawn once more and in my room, writing.

There is little to say. The room is nearly silent, the air strangely chill. Outside, dark birds are chattering as if to urge the sun to climb. Within there is but one light on and I am near it; pen, page and man within the small ellipsis of its glow.

Yesterday, ten thousand people died, more or less instantly, when a tidal wave swept across Sri Lanka. By nightfall, the number of reported dead had grown to twenty thousand. It is all but unimaginable: one moment, you are asleep in your bed and dreaming of pad Thai; the next you are submerged within the roiling contents of a giant washing machine, tossed about in random concussion with cars, desks, rosebushes, sharks and cattle, all the flotsam of our world.

The philosopher Nietzsche posited the "eternal recurrence of the same." In doing so he added to the realm of metaphysical possibilities what I have termed the "washing machine thesis." He said, in essence, that with the passage of sufficient time, every possible combination of matter must arise, indeed repeatedly so. Inevitably, he argued, given enough time, all the world's molecules must find themselves in precisely the same order, so that the same events, even the same beings, must recur, and lives be relived, street corners revisited, lines re-crossed. And then, like a washer on repeat cycle, it starts all over again.

It is indeed tempting to believe that locked within the All of space there is a finite amount of matter: planets, quarks, electrons, things like that. How can it be otherwise? What is, *is*—and surely what is is finite. If that is so, then the All amounts to a kind of massive washing machine in which all that stuff—all those elements of matter, those protons, neutrons and electrons— are endlessly recycled and *reused*.

Of course, there is another possibility. To some folks' minds, the amount of stuff is *not* finite: there is a source, a fountainhead, an exploding Prime Mover, if you will, spewing forth endless quantities of new material, new quarks, new stuff. This goes on forever. Space continues to expand. The All is not a closed system, but an open hand, a river that flows in all directions at once, with but a single organizing principle: it flows away.

Not one tidal wave, and not one sea. No ocean, and no shore. No seabed; nothing for the water to run back to. Molecules torn down to basics and dispersed like dandelion seeds into the infinite darkness of outer space; lives reduced to hydrogen and saline, then subsumed within the shoreless sea of being, never to return.

Scary, isn't it? Yet this image is far closer to the thinking of modern cosmologists than is

Nietzsche's washing machine thesis. It postulates that while there may be walls of the world of *human* experience, time and space are without bound, and no one has the right to expect one's molecules to be re-used in anything like a predictable fashion—if they are re-used at all.

Thoughts, though, do seem to rumble around inside a kind of washing machine of the mind. They disappear, lurk unseen in some dark corner for a small eternity, then reemerge. Lines are blurred; things get smeared together. Before you know it, Nietzsche is swirling underwater in Sri Lanka, and all the tidal waves of the world have simmered into the formless depths of space.

Jaipur

Roadkill

December 28, 2004

The sixteenth day began in mist, and with an armed guard at my patio door. I waved to him and he to me; we both smiled. Still, I wondered what was up. I had heard rumors about Bikram catching heat for leading us in yoga at the Taj Mahal, but that was all I knew.

Over breakfast, I confirmed that our yoga in the Taj had indeed sparked quite a controversy. We were the top headline on the cover of three newspapers, and made page two in several others. Apparently some Muslims believe that what we did was sacrilege, somehow defiled the Taj. They are outraged.

I later learned the reason for the guard

outside my door: I and all the other yogis were under house arrest.

On the other hand, there are those who applaud us. *The Hindustan Times,* for example, described our practice as "The first time the Taj has been used for a creative endeavor."

But now there is word that Bikram is about to be—or already has been—arrested. We reportedly broke a "Supreme Court Direction" by our practice at the Taj. Furthermore, rumor has it that when the authorities came for Bikram, he left for Delhi rather than face the charges. I wonder if he is holed up in the American Embassy at Shanti Path.

What is certain is that I have not seen Bikram in more than a day, and strain is showing on the face of Rajashree, his faithful wife, though she continues traveling with us. Tomorrow was supposed to be the start of Bikram's work with the cameramen for an upcoming special to be aired on *60 Minutes;* what will happen next is anyone's guess.

It was against this backdrop that my thoughts turned to Jaipur.

The road to Jaipur was quite bumpy, but nowhere near as bumpy as it was long, and only half as long as it was dangerous. A narrow, two-lane affair, it played host to every kind of swerving traffic, mechanical and mammalian; there were countless near-collisions, and several outright pile-ups, along the way.

Our own bus obliquely bumped against at least one bicyclist during the journey, and we ran a motorcyclist completely off the road; our intrepid driver didn't even stop.

Another highlight came when we very nearly killed an elderly pedestrian. The old man was propped up on a cane as he tried to ford the busy highway, but he was just too slow to cross in front of our bus, which was piloted by a madman. The whole world froze as we screeched to a bone-jarring halt and he hobbled off in double-time, his life spared.

Others were not so lucky. One especially memorable collision was the massively destructive head-on of two large trucks, one of which was carrying a load of chili peppers. Their crumpled front-ends were compressed like accordions, the noses of cartoon hammerhead sharks. Both vehicles had turned over, and ripe red peppers blanketed the road.

It is, in fact, almost impossible to convey in words the road conditions in India. Here is how the U.S. Department of State has put it:

> "Travel by road is dangerous…
>
> "Heavy traffic is the norm and includes (but is not limited to) overloaded trucks and buses, scooters, pedestrians, bullock and camel carts, horse or elephant riders *en route* to weddings, and free-roaming livestock.
>
> "If a driver hits a pedestrian or a cow, the vehicle and its occupants are at risk of being attacked by passersby. Such attacks pose significant risk of injury or death to the vehicle's occupants or at least incineration of the vehicle."

Almost all the day we pressed on, hurtling along the bumpy road to Jaipur.

"The World Endures But an Hour"
December 28, 2004

"The World is a bridge, pass over it... he who hopes for a day may hope for eternity; but the World endures but an hour."
— Christ (attributed); Inscription,
Muslim Mosque, Fatehpur Sikri

The highlight of the trip to Jaipur came when we stopped at Fatehpur Sikri, a palace built by order of the Mughal Emperor Akbar in 1571 as a new capital city to mark the glad occasion of his first son's birth. With its elaborate palace, formal courtyards, harems, tombs and mosque all carved from local red sandstone, it is truly spectacular; most authorities consider it the finest specimen of Mughal architecture in the world.

At a secluded corner of the courtyard, far away from the others, I encountered a very old man who took me aside and sold me—quite illegally, as I would learn later—four Mughal Empire-era coins. Thick and dirty, they bore the scars of time. When I asked him where he got them, he silently led me to a plowed field in a hidden part of the compound and pointed to the dirt. I gave him the money he wanted—a sum equivalent to less than twenty American dollars—and continued on my way.

The coins in my pocket, I walked the grounds of the royal city beneath a fiery sun. Massive red stones had been laid into plazas broad enough to stand an army, and the outer wall was punctuated with comely spires. It was easy to picture Mughal warriors gathering at the knee of the massive sandstone throne, their standards flying. I could almost hear the drums. But all these former denizens had vanished centuries ago, and today the only sounds were parrots poking out of random holes in the imperial barricades to shriek at me, and monkeys clattering along the rooftops. I stood alone at the farthest wall overlooking a vast saffron plain, watched an eagle carving the sky, and recalled the portico's inscription: *The world endures but an hour.*

We pressed on to Jaipur, ascending to its plateaued heights through craggy mountain passes pocked with clusters of unbearably emaciated children. We were bound for the luxurious Rajputana Palace Hotel; ah, the irony of it all.

When at last we reached the hotel, I was able to read the day's news.

It was bad. *The Rajastan Times* now reported 25,000 dead by tidal wave in Sri Lanka, the Maldives and southern India.

"Graves have been dug for mass burials," said the article, entitled *Bracing for Epidemic,* "even as wailing women scour dismembered corpses on the beach for loved ones."

But an hour.

Pink City, Amber Fort
December 29, 2004

Dawn broke in Jaipur to the sound of myriad screaming parrots, and my curtains parted on a gorgeous, crystalline day. I showered and moved out promptly for the city center with the other yogis. It was bustling, and I liked its energy immediately.

Founded in 1727 by the astronomer-king Sawai Jai Singh, Jaipur often is referred to as the "Pink City"; it was first painted pink at the time of its establishment, probably to evoke the indigenous red sandstone of nearby Mughal palaces—an echo of Fatehpur Sikri. But when, in 1863, Jaipur's residents dressed themselves in pink to welcome Prince Albert to their city, Jaipur's reputation as the Pink City was cemented forever. Since then, most construction here has been in pink.

After a brief driving tour of the city proper, we made north through tenements and shanty towns, roughly following the course of a wide, slow river. At the base of the mountain we abandoned the bus and ascended, first by pickup truck and then on foot, into the heights of the medieval Rajput citadel of Amber.

Named for the unusual golden stones of which it is constructed, Amber Fort was the capital of the Kachwaha people for six centuries before the birth of Jaipur. It is ancient—an inscription on one of the pillars of the Sun Temple inside the Fort dates to 945 A.D.—and every successive ruler to occupy the stronghold seems to have procured additions to its beauty. Today it is a place of breathtaking views, the complex chambers and passageways of an enormous harem, and Sheesh Mahal, considered by many to be the finest hall of mirrors in the world.

I climbed the several hundred steps to the top of a range of craggy hills and entered the Fort proper. From here I could take the view of the Chambal River, ochre and serpentine in the distance; three giant, muddy elephants were bathing at the cat-tailed water's edge. I moved a few steps forward, intersecting with a band of tourist college students who demanded that I pose with them for a picture or two—I, ever the oddity—then ascended yet another set of steep stone stairs. Here I passed an ancient-looking man wearing thick glasses and a colorful turban, lying aground and plinking away at a hoary, hand-made instrument that produced a beleaguered, squinched tone. *Twang. Twang. Twang-twang-twang.*

Then an outstretched hand, begging.

I moved into the section of the palace dedicated to the housing of the master's harem; it was damnably hot. The walls were adorned with frescoes showing groups of women interacting happily, pouring water out of pitchers, things like that. Doors to each woman's individual bed-chamber opened on a central plaza where they no doubt gathered during the day; but a guide showed how another hidden passageway gave private access to each of the rooms from the other side. Moving along literally within the walls, the master was invisible; only his consort for the evening could be certain of his choosing. The tunnel was specifically designed to prevent the wives from guessing who the master might be visiting on any given night. Thus, it was explained to me, was peace maintained.

Squinting, I entered the shadowy hall of mirrors. Little shards of brilliantly reflective glass were set in every inch of the walls and ceiling; to light a candle here would be to fire a galaxy. But it was dark, so dark today, the absence of celebrants palpable, lugubrious, evoking the carnage of time. I much preferred the sunlight.

Outside it was a golden day, and I spent the rest of it riding a colorfully painted elephant around the Fort, hanging onto a wooden frame strapped to the animal's back as its giant haunches rose and fell beneath me. And I sat awhile in the grass at the bottom of the mountain, near a wizened-looking sage who seemed entranced in meditation, and watched the sluggish river flow away.

On the trip back into Jaipur, we stopped and took a distant view of Jal Mahal, a majestic lake palace arising from broad, silent waters that spread without a ripple as far as I could see.

We took our lunch at the palace of Jaipur's living Maharaja. Amazingly, and quite by chance, I met him face to face.

It happened this way: I was returning for a second bowl of channa masala when a little child, a girl of five or six, waved to me from behind an intricately latticed gate. I waved back; she smiled. I walked over to her. She acted very shy, but didn't seem to want me to leave, either. Then the Maharaja himself appeared behind the screen, walked over to his granddaughter, sister of the heir to his throne, and led her gently away.

I spent the evening wandering the streets of Jaipur alone and on foot, surrounded as always by throngs of smiling, emaciated children, and followed, often as not, by a lone flea-bitten dog.

When night fell, thick cloud-cover blotted out the moon, and I joined the other yogis for a dinner served in carnival atmosphere an hour south of the town. We drank beer and watched the spectacle unfold: henna-handed ladies danced with kettles balanced ten high on their heads; men walked barefoot on red-hot coals in the inky blackness of a night torn only by the sparks arising from the embers beneath them. And, in the distance, the primal sound of drums.

Then it began: a boy of about eight repeatedly drew large quantities of hydrocarbons into his mouth and blew out massive plumes of flame, the radiance of which cast everything in garish, horrid light. Trees became black lines that fractured the suddenly magenta sky; the dancers became planar, floating dimensionless above an unseen pediment. In an instant, the dragon's breath expired and everything receded to black, as though the light he cast was but a liquid tide drawn back into the shoreless depths of space.

The boy's father sat quietly at the edge of the ring, his face carved by shadows, smiling darkly.

Coins, and the Realm
December 30, 2004

What day is it? It hardly matters anymore. The news is almost eighty thousand dead. Appreciation of the tidal wave's true devastation grows daily. Ten thousand of the dead are Southern Indians; their bodies are being burned *en masse* in Tamil Nadu, the province next to Kerela, where I now plan to go.

Today I simply rested, walking up a rocky, trash-piled street amid a throng of filthy children to a gem purveyor's shop. Jaipur, mired in poverty, ironically is famous for its precious stones.

Here, despite the squalor of the outer world, were brilliant sapphires, topaz, tourmalines and gold; every useless bauble you could conjure. A jovial, corpulent man squatted over an open furnace and hammered metal into rings; he smiled as I walked blankly away from the place, preferring the hard reality of the street.

Around the corner, I stopped and bought a large bag of dried potatoes for three kids who had been following me. They were so happy they looked like they might cry. But within seconds they set to fighting over their prize, and after a brief and futile effort to encourage sharing, I walked away, saddened.

Even this day of rest was not without incident. Remember those Mughal coins I bought from the old man at Fatehpur Sikri? Today they came back to haunt me when I tried to send them home along with several other things by Federal Express. The shipping clerk inspected the box before it was sealed and said nothing of the coins. Incredibly, he then went to his office, ripped open the box, and searched it again without my knowledge. Finding the coins, he returned to the hotel and demanded I present myself at the front desk. I met him there.

I decided my best defense would be a kind of offense, so I acted intensely offended that he had deigned to open my box. This was easy to do, because I *was* offended; I had had everything carefully packed, but when I looked inside the box now, it was evident its contents had been ransacked by uncaring hands. Even the two small packages of incense had been opened, their contents rifled. I feigned outrage, abruptly grabbed my box and hastily left. There was nothing he could do; I can, when tasked, move quickly.

But the truth is, I was worried. As I hurried away from the man, scenes from *Midnight Express* flitted across the movie screen of my mind, and I imagined the years I might spend chained in some forgotten corner of an Indian prison for so trifling a thing.

As I write this now, I am ensconced within

the snowy interior of a chartered jet, hurtling due east towards Kolkata (Calcutta), and thankful to be out of Jaipur without incident. It is ten p.m., and I am very hungry, ready for almost any food that comes.

None did. We touched down after midnight, empty and worn, and were greeted at the airport by an upbeat (and obviously unjailed) Bikram. He hugged us excitedly and handed out roses. It seemed a tacit apology. But it was obvious that, in his mind at least, the incident at the Taj Mahal was behind him.

When I stepped outside the terminal and into the dark, at once I sensed the invisible presence of a new, even more pernicious pollution. Within minutes of boarding the bus that would take us to the hotel, we yogis—seasoned travelers who had by now become hardened to even the most lung-searing contamination— were hacking and covering our faces with whatever we could find. But nothing helped. Our eyes burned with a maddening new fire, and tears streaked our cheeks.

The bus ride through the black streets of

Calcutta seemed never to end, and took us past places where dozens of shadowy bodies lay motionless at the roadside. *Could it be*, I wondered, *that so many spend their nights on the ground, without even a mat or a blanket?* The poverty looked cruel, even in the charitable obscurity of darkness.

Two hours later—hours spent weaving through the labyrinthine city, staring out the window at cryptic horrors shrouded in gloom—we reached our lodgings. Now too nauseous to eat, and strangely bone-weary, I lay down without protest in a very moldy bed, covering my face with a towel, and exited to sleep.

Calcutta

His Repertoire
December 31, 2004

I awoke to another dawn and peered out at what I could see of Calcutta. It wasn't much. Thick pollution totally obscured the view beyond a quarter mile. Even after weeks in India, I was amazed. The city was trapped inside a lung-searing cloud.

I was late to reach the group's bus and it departed without me, so I headed into Calcutta on foot and alone. Knowing the yogis' proclivity for tourist attractions and hoping to intersect with them, I struck out first for Victoria Memorial Hall, frequently wiping the soot that accumulated at the corners of my mouth. I crossed a bridge, passed a place where obviously homeless girls were disemboweling a small chicken, pulling at its stringy entrails with their bare fingers. Across the street, two men were trying to lift a giant irrigation pipe. Suddenly they hoisted it, revealing a length of more than thirty feet, and staggered away.

I approached Victoria Memorial Mall. A completely naked beggar sprawled in the grass that ringed the place, his hair matted as old wool, his back streaked with long black stains. Women in colorful saris were busy constructing a road nearby, walking back and forth with stacks of bricks and buckets of concrete mix balanced on their heads. A pale sun bore down through the blinding pollution.

The Hall was a large museum of paintings and artifacts from colonial India. Poking out like icebergs among the obligatory topographs, rifles and pith helmets, were several fascinating paintings by Jamini Roy. But the pinnacle of the exhibition was an utterly spectacular painting of the Mahishasura Mardini Durga, the Hindu goddess demon-slayer, rendered in oil by an unknown artist.

The yogis nowhere to be found, I wandered

back outside and followed the course of the Hooghly River's eastern bank a few miles, making my way towards the mad bazaar at New Market.

En route, I ducked into an exhibition at the Government College of Art and Craft, 28 Jawaharlal Nehru Road, and for three rupees—approximately one and one-third cents—saw some truly fantastic art.

These were the ultramodern images of Calcutta's youthful avant-garde—a man standing on the precipice of suicide, a brain sliced in two by a knife—displayed amid a sculpture garden lit by naked bulbs.

At last I reached New Market, a pulsating mass of humanity swarming together as one. People shoved and pushed against me, horns blared and the pungent smell of burning foodstuffs filled the air. There was nowhere to simply *be*, nowhere to stand still, even for an instant.

Drawn further into the marketplace by the energy of the crowd, I came upon some of the most pathetic, desperate human beings I had yet encounted: severely deformed beggars lying at the gutter. I passed one man whose torso was so small it could have fit inside a shoebox. He had no legs at all, and only one arm. This he raised in my direction, eyes tearing through me like drillbits. I walked past him, continuing on my way for fifty feet or so, then involuntarily froze. The crowd swirled around me, helter-skelter in my suddenly columnar midst. It didn't matter if they broke themselves against me. I had become an island in a thrashing sea.

Never once had I yet given to a beggar in India. But here I turned around, fought my way back, and gave him not a little but everything I had. I had seen the whole of his repertoire, all that he could do. For him to have any hope of survival in a world like ours, the one thing of which he was capable—raising a single trembling hand—had to be enough. It had to be enough to reach me, to take hold of my soul. It *had* to be.

Here was a force beyond resistance, a law of physics disguised in a beggar's rags.

Hear the Bass Drum
December 31, 2004

Despite the corpses burning at Tamil Nadu, despite the more than one hundred thousand souls drowned in the Indian Ocean and Arabian Sea, despite the circumstances of the maimed and destitute sleeping in the streets around us, we yogis rang in the New Year with drinking, eating beyond satiation, and ample good cheer. Life is like that, you know? *Smile and the world smiles with you,* the saying goes, *cry and you cry alone.* Writing at my table afterwards, merely to describe the abject poverty of our hedonistic myopia nearly makes me weep. Yet to do other than we did would be unthinkable. For there is no overcoming the darkness that surrounds us, no way to ignite the stillborn stars whose candles never glimmered in the sapphire skies of life, and to attempt such a thing, or even to bemoan its impossibility, is to succumb. We must go on. We must celebrate what is, as it is, while it is.

Thus it was that at midnight, January 1, 2005,

I could be found on stage, behind a drum kit, doing what I do best: living. Two other yogis and I had taken over the arena, pushing aside a geriatric Hindu band and firing up some red-hot American blues.

The result was startling. It was as if a drove of wild animals had been sprung from a cage. In an instant, forty dancing hedonists appeared before us. Hands went up; drinks were passed like life preservers on a boiling sea. Purple footlights cut the night. Sweaty bodies pulsed and twisted with biologic urgency.

Outside in the dark, I knew, just beyond the hotel's heavy gate, lay men and women starving, armless, legless. Even as I pounded out the beat, I thought of them. What was the depth of their vacancy, I wondered? Were they not hopeless? Were they devoid even of *dreams?* And through it all my right leg, muscular and perfect as any a human being has ever had the joy to call his own, hammered out the steady beating of the bass drum, at once the tight quintessence of the rhythmic trance in which the dancers' sticky bodies swayed, and at the same time a wandering, disembodied ghost that echoed through the streets of shadowy Calcutta far beyond the edges of the stage. Almost without my urging, it kept pounding and pounding, on and on and on...

Sighting Everest
January 1, 2005

Dawn came, and with it the sovereignty of suffering, the ascendancy of pain. At once I knew it: an artist speaks not merely for himself, but everyone. His is the voice of every creature that has ever been, and ever will be. It is not enough to sing out the tones of one's solitary life; the duty is to plunge into the oneness of being and bring forth its essence, talismanic and affirmed.

Within the fragile interlude of my own candle of existence lies but one hope: authentic expression. And though my destination is oblivion, this alone is worth aspiring to: authenticity in life, in love, and in death—the Everest of being.

Walking in Calcutta,
we share a secret, you and I;
a smile that crosses oceans,
seals continents inside a little jar.

I act like I know this place,
what I'm doing here,
but I don't;
yet our exchange confirms
it doesn't really matter.

Walking in Calcutta, I am called to speak for you:
every being who has ever lived
and ever will be
speaks through me.

It is not my soul that seeks its voice,
but life, life itself
finding and expressing its essence.

The Origin of a Species
January 1, 2005

It needn't surprise you to learn that I have discovered a new species here in India: *homosapiens restroomicus*—restroom man.

You may not know it, but there are human

beings in this world whose sole occupational object is the upkeep of a loo. Here is a man whose life is played out entirely within the artificial half-light of a restroom, amid the Vitreous Hindware and other necessaries of the place; as far as I can tell, except to eat and sleep, he never leaves. I have seen such a fellow in the earliest morn, then returned at midnight for a leak to find the same poor soul still there. You would not think such a thing is possible, but this is India.

Do not mistake my affect for a denigration of this man's profession; nothing could be further from the truth of my intent. For here is a being so attuned to the sights and sounds of his workplace, so Zen-like in the resoluteness of his focus, that he can diagnose from the timbre of the flushing of a urinal the impending failure of a tiny rubber washer buried deep within its guts—before it occurs. Here is a man who keeps his workplace as pristine as the Alps. I have seen fully restored '57 Chevys that were nowhere near as shiny and clean. When you wash your hands and a few droplets fall upon the marble altar of his sanctuary, he wipes them away with an energy that can only be described as giving glory to God. And the beauty of it all, of course, is that this is a room full of toilets.

His chief problem is boredom. For between the patrons—pissing and shitting and setting the general preconditions for his existence—there is lots of time. Little eons, I imagine; small eternities. I have even observed a certain happiness, a kind of exhilaration really, when somebody makes a mess: each wayward droplet, every hand towel on the floor, represents minutes filled, purpose reconfirmed, existence sanctified.

Clockwork
January 1, 2005

The movements of the yogis are glacial: load them into a bus and soon they are spilling out again, drifting back to their rooms or disappearing altogether in the madness of the street. Tell our group it is time to leave and few of us move at all. It has become something of a joke with us: if we are asked to get on the bus, most of us just sit there, letting the very few obedient souls go as told; if they eventually give up and come back, we know the instruction to depart was indeed premature. We use them like scouts, an advance team. And on the rare occasions when they do not return, we know that, yes, it is time to finish our coffees, go to the restroom, gather our things, and gradually leave. But still there is no urgency. For all concerned, I suppose, it has been like lumbering along in mud.

After an inevitably long span of time—time enough to build the pyramids, then watch them disintegrate into the dusts of infinitude—our motley crew boarded another antiquated bus. We were supposed to be going to Mother Theresa's Mission, but we went no further than a thousand feet before traffic ground to a halt.

We sat in that position for something close to an hour, kinetic rivulets of pedestrians and animals of every kind swarming around the bus's paralyzed behemoth corpse. The sun beat down on the battered metal breadbox that contained us; windows were flung open, pried open, or cursed. In through every portal rolled the caustic, sooty air to which we had become accustomed. I was drenched in bitter sweat.

Boredom set in, that species of boredom so mature you catch yourself absently poking about in overhead storage lockers that are not your own. This is an unconscious act; it is not as though you can reasonably expect their contents to include anything of interest, but there you are. I opened the locker nearest me, and in it, sitting upright and facing me as though on some sort of display, was an art deco clock. You could have asked me to guess the contents of that locker for a thousand years, and I would never have said, "Clock." Duffle bag? Sure. Fire extinguisher? Maybe. But a *clock?* It was, in fact, the last thing in the world I expected to see. But of course there it was: the last thing in the world I expected to see, in the last place I expected to see it. It could have been the avatar for all of India.

The clock, this random crew of bus-bound

yogis. I couldn't tell you how, but it was all starting to make sense. Things fit together like pieces of a puzzle. The contours of events became a little visible, and could be rendered seamless by a willing mind. It was as if some unperceived Rosetta Stone had turned one click, opening a vista to the truth of life. Everything was absurd, and there was nothing at all to wonder at. The thought scared me.

Another little piece of my illusion had silently fluttered away.

Mecca
January 1, 2005

We drove on, lost beyond recapture in the maddening scrum. Calcutta showed herself enormous, maddeningly Byzantine, populous almost beyond belief. Thousands of people filled every square mile. Crowds poured across trembling, desiccated bridges spanning rivers of mire, streamed helter-skelter into slums so jammed that human beings and animals occupied every conceivable space. Things veered and skidded in all directions, howled and ran abruptly into the road. Our vehicle lurched forward, screeched to a halt, and poked ahead again, the silence of my awe broken time to time by the din of something—or someone—crashing against the battered aluminum flanks of the bus.

We came, an hour hence, to a street lined with palms. It was strangely quiet here—eerily so. Not a single parrot, monkey or man could be seen or heard. A feeble breeze toyed lazily with the hot, thick air but turned no leaf. The only movement was a foot-long rat that crept along the gutter.

A few paces ahead, and up a narrow flight of concrete stairs, were the yoga rooms of Bishnu Ghosh, Bikram's guru and the brother of Paramhansa Yogananda. The whole voyage had been a kind of pilgrimage, I saw, and this was nearly Mecca.

"Nearly?" I can almost hear you saying. What could be more sacred to a Bikram disciple than the place young Bikram first discovered yoga,

found his guru, trained? This was hallowed ground, surely. Today photographs of Bikram in his prime as yoga champion of all of India adorned the sweat-streaked walls, but one could still discern an ancient echo of the penniless young Bikram, tired, sore, yet ever dedicated, clawing his way through the slums to climb the steep red stairs and practice yet again.

But, yes, it must be said that this was *nearly* Mecca, for within two hours we were in the boyhood home of Yogananda himself, the very root of modern yoga's journey to the West and a shrine to meditation and enlightenment. It was a ray of hope, a sacred place that effused a powerful spiritual presence.

The home itself was bare and clean, evoking the simplicity of a monastic Sparta. But the aura that enfolded it was rich, powerful, *alive*. Entering, I felt stripped of every possession I had ever claimed, or even desired. It was like taking toys away from a child: all the things I did not need were gently put beyond my reach. And it was so obvious: none of them mattered. For in these windowless rooms, with barely so much as a light bulb, Yogananda had attained enlightenment. The beacon of his power still remained within the walls of his tiny meditation chamber, pulsating with an energy only Van Gogh could paint.

The group fell all but silent in the presence, and slowly made its humbled way back out into the street. But I stayed behind, lingering in a kind of anteroom, mesmerized by the surreal, whispered purring of a large black cat. Naked sunlight beat down through an opening above, streaking the floor; a fountain dribbled quietly somewhere nearby. The cat moved from the shadows to sprawl at my feet in the shard of light, its glossy fur suddenly ablaze with bolts of color.

He turned over. Amber eyes with diamond-shaped obsidian pupils held my gaze. I heard the briefest flutter of wings, caught the shadow of something moving in the open space above. The cat seemed almost to smile, an expression that sent a shiver through me. Then it arose and slowly sauntered away, its haunches rawboned as a lioness, the curl of its tail arcing like a question mark that disappeared around the corner of a cinderblock wall, leaving me alone again in the column of light. Only the gentle lapping sound of the water remained.

I stayed lost in all that I had felt and seen at Yogananda's house until our bus heaved up at Mother Teresa's Mission, 54A Acharya Jagadish Chandra Bose Road.

The nondescript building that houses the mission fronts on a busy, polluted thoroughfare, and could only be entered through a narrow concrete alleyway. With irony not lost on me, a couple of children missing limbs panhandled just outside its gate. I stepped past them and into the antechamber of the mission. *"Let us love each person—the unborn, the young, the old, the sick and the poor..."* a sign proclaimed; this was the hand-scrubbed simplicity of Mother Teresa's message.

We toured the premises, taking in a small museum of simple artifacts pertaining to the mission's founding. Then we were allowed to wander more freely. Going off alone again, I came to the perimeter of the ward. Here an arrow of sunlight reached the spigot where a nun bent down to fill a wooden pail; the water glistened like mercury for an instant, then vanished with the wince of the handle turned. A glorious being raised herself, the blue and white of her raiment framing a wrinkled face imbued with the awesome power of unconditional love.

There is a magnificence in real dedication, in adherence to a noble purpose, that eclipses so-called beautiful things. Carrying water, tending to the surpassing requirements of the ward, these nuns were the embodiment of that transcendence.

Here amid the chaos, disease and poverty of Calcutta, Mother Teresa had founded a refuge for the most forsaken souls: the homeless, poor and dying. This was, for most, a final destination, the last stop on a spur of rail terminating at the lowest point of hell—a train that ran one way. Her nuns had dedicated their lives to the alleviation of this agony, even if only at the meagerest of margins. They ministered, I knew, to the incessant draining of wounds and changing of bandages, wiped away uncontrolled feces and waged a tireless war against the onslaught of bacteria, insects and other vermin. But most of all they held hands, stroked foreheads, and gazed into eyes containing only the weakest fires of life. The many thousands they could not save were comforted in dying, eased into the dark and silent waters that lead to the sea.

Among Gods
January 2, 2005

If, as has been said, a stint in India will beat the restlessness out of any wanderer, a few days spent walking the slums of Calcutta will all but beat out the spark of one's life.

The feeling came on slowly. Even on the morning of the final day, things seemed okay. I could be found wandering the streets, poking my head in here and there, trying to avoid aggressive vendors and generally taking in the multiplicity of life. But by the time the day had drawn to an end, I was fractured, trembling, lost.

It began mundanely enough: with equipment failure. The charger for my camera suddenly burned up. Then the battery itself promptly ran down. This meant I could no longer take a single picture, nor could I upload images to the web. It was a serious issue, and something I needed to confront head-on.

I tried to isolate the problem, but without a multimeter my efforts were wasted. Two electricians, amiable fellows who worked for the hotel, got deeply involved in my plight, and without a fee; together we found the offending circuit, but it was beyond repair.

My next step, naturally, was to try to find a replacement part. You might well laugh at me, it was such a fool's errand; a Minolta BC-200 battery charger could no more be procured in Calcutta than could a platypus. But I was determined to solve the problem, and set out to replace the charger or, in the worst case, the camera itself.

Thus began an epic journey which would end, many hours later, in the black market of Khidirpur Road.

I began at Sony World, finding there a camera that cost a thousand dollars and could not accept my memory card; this was at best a last-ditch option. I moved on to the so-called Forum, an upscale mall where I had been told there were cameras in abundance, but searched every store in the place to discover not a single one. My trip to the Forum, though, did yield another illustration of that peculiar marketing genius which is solely Indian. Calcutta's first and only multicultural food court, a sign informed me cheerily, bore the appellation "BURP."

I carried on across town to the so-called Esplanade. Why it is named that is beyond imagination: there was no open pavement, no promenade and no shoreline. Instead, I was swallowed by another jumbled sprawl of smoky eateries packed with animals and men. It was another place where cameras were reputedly as common as housecats, but go there, my friend, and you will discover they are nowhere to be found. All I left with was an increasing belief in the futility of my mission.

I was urged on to Chandy Market, a rambling

maze of merchants packed so tightly into a squalorous side-street that I was almost afraid to enter it. Here was another maze of battered storefronts, broken-down pushcarts, begrimed eateries and haggled transactions. After braving my way to a dead-end that put me in mind of the terminus of a diseased intestine, I was again rebuffed: it was another place wholly devoid of cameras.

"To Metro Galley," I was told, but in going there I only lost another hour, descending into a narrow alleyway filthy enough to enthrall a bacteriologist for life, and emerging with nothing but disinfectant in my hands.

Everywhere I went, people kept whispering a dark refrain: "Khidirpur." Calcutta's black market, I was given to understand, was a place capable of supplying anything I could possibly imagine. *Khidirpur.* I tried to resist its siren call, but in the end, I proved too weak.

Now at this point you may be tempted to suppose I have a death-wish, but nothing could be further from the truth. It was not an urge to die, nor even to take chances, that drew me into the recesses of Calcutta's black market, but the undeniable impulse to fully live. I had to see for myself what went on there.

It was a long hike from the central sprawl of the city where I had squandered most of the morning; to get to the place, I had to trek through several kilometers of warehouses and run-down factories evocative of Sinclair's *The Jungle*. There was no sign marking the entrance, and I found it half by chance, reading the ambiguous vacillations of the human swarm.

I entered the dark hallway with trepidation, the blood in my carotid arteries roaring. Fluorescent lights hummed and flickered above, casting an illicit glare. Goods were mounded floor to ceiling: Persian carpets, crates of foodstuffs, bolts of cloth.

Cages of swaying cobras.

Hallways shot off in all directions, nearly occluded by vendibles. I chose one and followed its winding course deeper into the maze of money and men.

I reached a central chamber. The noise was deafening as people cried their bids and argued over prices, their voices merging like a synthesis of jungle insects to an almost mechanical drone. I was within the matrix of a giant hive, each vendor's cubicle a hexagon of nectar for the horde.

I caught a whiff of the waxy effluvium of electronics equipment and made my way towards it, finding a stall of radios and similar merchandise. There I displayed my broken camera and was led directly to a camera vendor.

He was a young man, and suitably optimistic about selling me something—anything, it seemed—but among his myriad wares was only one thing I could use: a Nikon Coolpix 3200. It was capable of reading my memory card and connecting to computer via USB, and as such was the full solution to my problem. For this he wanted the equivalent of two hundred bucks.

It seemed awfully cheap, and I was suspicious. I made him charge it up, turn it on, take pictures, do cartwheels, stand on his head. Everything worked.

Getting him to give me all the standard accessories, however, proved to be like frisking a shy girl—he had them hidden here and there in various drawers and other out-of-the way places, and yielded each part unwillingly. But in the end, I had the whole of what I needed: Camera? Check. Charger? Check. USB cable? Check. Batteries? Check. I was good to go.

There was only one problem: the money. All my currency now lay before the black marketeer, but it was not enough. Still, the nearly nine thousand rupees I did possess was a lot of cash in this afflicted corner of the globe, and skinny men around us started taking notice of it. I became acutely aware of every glance and gesture, increasingly convinced that it was time for me to go.

Perhaps sensing my apprehension, the vendor abruptly proposed an accom-modation: he would give me the camera, but his brother would shadow me all the way to my hotel. There I would cash a traveler's check, pay him the deficit, and send him hiking back to Khidirpur.

It was a strange proposal, but easy to accept under the circumstances. The dark-faced brother posed no threat to me; he was little more than a child. And indeed he followed me at a discrete distance all the many miles to the hostelry, received his brother's money with a tight-lipped smile, and returned without a word to the anonymity of the street.

Camera in hand and batteries charged, I knew in my bones that the time had come: I had to go to the poorest part of the city.

But I was *so* exhausted. Surreal reality and metamorphic dreams had been bleeding into one, and the truth is, my mind never rested. Shocking images, sounds and smells bombarded me with the relentless, grating frequency of a hundred paparazzi's flashbulbs. Everywhere I went I was overstimulated: faces popped up from all sides, their eyes wide and staring. Endless hands reached out for me. Solicitors ceaselessly solicited.

I fared no better in sleep. There I was assaulted by an army of nightmares: the leper girls, the boy with dying legs, the urchins pleading, the corpse rotting at the edge of the street. Bears, boars, headless chickens and misproportioned beggars peopled my dreams. All the while, untold scores of weird bacteria were gnawing away at me.

This had gone on for weeks. Through it all, I had remained on edge, ever vigilant to my surroundings. My heart-pounding descent into the penetralia of the black market had been only the most recent super-stimulus. Part of me had had all that I could take. And yet I knew—*I knew*—I could never leave Calcutta until I had been to the worst of its slums.

I had eight hours left—far too little time to walk the distance I needed to cover—so I hired a cabbie to drive me into North Calcutta. He was a man with very definite ideas about what to do with my time, a fact which annoyed me initially but later turned out to be a godsend. He showed me the sanitarium—I can't even *imagine* what goes on in there—and the prison, where he told me the terrorists are housed. Then we headed for Kashipur, Barangar and Nandan Nagar, close to the toxic river. It was the place agreed upon by all: the darkest heart of the city. There I got out and walked.

Calcutta is home to more than fourteen

million people, and is one of the poorest, most densely populated cities in the world. Thirty thousand souls occupy every square kilometer of ground. Ponder that: we're talking about sixty thousand people crammed into each square mile. And fully two-thirds of the population lives in slums, the so-called Bustees, in primitive huts made out of clay, corrugated iron and scraps of wood. Nine and a half million of them.

These, however, are the *privileged* ones. Less fortunate still are the squatters, who live in cloth and plastic shelters anywhere they can.

But the worst of all is reserved for the million or so who possess only a bent tin bowl and dirt-encrusted mat. Their wandering existence is played out on the pavement, in doorways, under ox-pulled carriages, in garbage dumps and in competition with pigs and feral dogs. These were my hosts today.

The first thing to notice, for me at least, was the garbage. Calcutta is full of filth, simply *full* of it; but here I was entering an area that had the characteristic of seeming to be one large mound, mile after mile, of trash. Sure, things poked up out of it. Buildings, for example. And a river ran through it. But to me the character of the place, its essence if you will, was that of a large and toxic dump.

I was confronted by souls who never left here, people whose lives, from birth to death, were played out amid the garbage heaps. I saw a child fighting a pig over a piece of trash. I saw three children struggling ferociously, bodies mired in the gooey mounds of rotting detritus, faces black with grime. They were competing over the contents of a newly emptied garbage pail.

Just down a narrow alleyway, I came upon a sideshow that could have been a metaphor for all of life, and perhaps was: a child tightrope walker. She was a girl of maybe seven, balancing with all the concentration of a dying monk ten feet above the hard-packed ground and watchful crowd. She crossed a loosely slung rope, first on bare feet, then astride a bicycle wheel's rim, and finally shuffling along atop her bent food pan. As if that weren't enough, she also balanced stacks of brass cups on her head. She was doing what it took to eke out a survival. Despite all this, she didn't look well-fed.

I moved on, tracking north along the eastern edge of the Hooghly River. Dark smoke floated sullenly above a large, dilapidated building up ahead. Drawing nearer, I saw that the smoke was from the burning of human remains; the building was a Hindu crematorium.

I was pushing through a tightly packed throng of beggars, now all but oblivious to the hundreds of hands that reached out to touch my shoulders, arms and face, somehow at peace with the sea of eyes that poured their vision into me— as though I were a bottomless vessel able to receive the infinite torrent of their dreams. They were eyes that somehow made one face, the way fishes make one school, the way snowflakes make one storm. Eyes as indecipherable and countless as the raindrops of the monsoon.

I struggled through the mob, reached the crematorium's entrance and stepped inside. A half-darkness, the pallor of death, pervaded the place. Corpses littered the floor, strewn with ceremonial marigolds. Incense hung thick and pungent, blackening the air. I coughed, and thought about tuberculosis.

Here were ten emaciated bodies at my feet, but it was I who was of interest; the whole room of mourners suddenly turned towards me and drew nearer, all but forgetting the corpses. Smoke of incense filled my nostrils with a stifling intensity; a naked flame danced somewhere in a distant corner of the room. My head spun. I staggered, felt my body falling away like a winter coat.

Suddenly the cabbie burst upon the scene and grabbed my arm, jarring me back to my senses. I was ushered into the street, but it too was packed with dirty bodies, another hundred people who would drink me with their eyes, touch me with their hands...

At last I reached the muddy eastern bank of the Hooghly River. Here dying sunlight—bent by smog into a silver fraction of its natural radiance—painted floating trash and bathers alike in caliginous gloom. I couldn't believe that anyone would choose to immerse himself in such fetid waters, but there they were:

nearly naked men, women and children by the hundreds, up to their necks in water that contained dead animals, floating rubbish, and the giant rainbow streaks of industrial waste.

Across the river in the distance behind them, a tableau of back-nosed factories with jutting towers belched plumes of smoke. It was the essence of industrial apocalypse, and in its foreground swam the children of the ancient, simple Earth, still striving for the humblest joys of ordinary life. Sustenance, fellowship. Even love. I stared as though I had beheld Medusa and been turned to stone. Then I became aware that someone behind me was honking.

My cabbie had become increasingly impatient with his customer. I couldn't say whether it was the advance of twilight or the unwavering trajectory of our journey ever deeper into the slums—but he was blowing his horn impatiently and motioning with his arm for me to hurry along.

I got in and urged the driver ahead, directing him into a narrow track clogged with totally destitute people. We inched forward, deeper into the crush, until at last he begged to turn back. Assuming I would assent, he at once began a turning maneuver. But I did not assent. Instead, I pressed him onward. He warned me sternly that the taxi might become swamped in the living bodies, immobile amid the clamoring souls. But here was the leading edge of my experience. To go forward was the reason I came.

There have been several times in the course of these notes when I have been tempted to simply throw up my hands and say that words cannot communicate what I beheld. I have resisted the impulse, not wanting to concede the failure. But here I must come dangerously close, for it is true: some things simply must be experienced to be believed.

I struggle to convey the barbarous hues of even their dwellings, gray as the color of soot, smeared by random violence with the blackened streaks of tallow grease, founded on rotting trash.

These were, quite frankly, places you would not consent to enter for a second; it is all but impossible to conceive that millions of our fellow human beings are consigned to live in such conditions their entire lives. And this is to say nothing of the people themselves.

It was the looks on their faces—the awe at seeing blue-eyed, Western me in the slum, the weariness of the weight of their existences, the resignation to raw destiny—that grabbed my spine and shook me to my core.

Splintered, pale light weighed down by dense contaminants like smoke from burning garbage was what outwardly lighted their expressions; yet, here and there I glimpsed the inward fire of life, life on the thinnest edge of being, life against all odds. And here, I tell you from my innermost soul, was the cuttingest thing of all: the light within them was so beautiful to see. It was breathtaking, impossible. It was an orchid blooming in Antarctica, and I knew I was among gods.

How do you at once recoil in horror and yet weep tears of joy? How do you shudder at the wretched stench of putrid waste while in the same breath beholding with absolute clarity the purest beauty you have ever seen? I tell you it is wrenching, a duality that drives you deeper into your questions even as you instinctively retreat.

Many hours after the driver said goodbye, images of their faces brazed my mind's eye. I was so beaten—the total experience of Calcutta had drained me so completely—that I became suddenly ill. I was nauseous, dizzy. My stomach churned and ached, and my spine throbbed from the base of my neck to my tailbone. I was miserable. Then I thought of the people of North Calcutta and realized I felt nothing. I smiled, lay down in a fairly clean bed, and closed my eyes.

But terrible images roiled within me. In fact, with my eyes closed, they were *more* intense. No matter what I tried to think about, I saw huge mounds of trash, people crawling in trash, smelled trash. It seemed I too was rotting on the inside. Rot: that is the closest I can come to telling you what I felt.

And I have never been so tired. Not after I got out of Africa at the end of a 150-mile footrace though the Sahara Desert. Not after the Boston Marathon, or even my qualifying run, the 3:08 Marine Corps Marathon that was, without question, the prime athletic achievement of my life. Not after getting trapped on Denali and severely exposed in a freezing, sleepless rain. Not even after the forty-mile ultramarathon around Canandaigua Lake in upstate New York, the one that damn near killed me.

Never.

Here was a feeling of disease, confusion, dizziness and stench I simply couldn't shake. It was as though something foreign had taken up residence inside me. I could think only of what I had seen, heard and smelled; every other thought was beyond me. I stood on unsure legs. I wanted to vomit, even though I had not eaten. I wanted to cry, but couldn't let the tears flow: I couldn't take what the release of emotions would have done to my body. I was too damn weak for it.

Calcutta must be among the most intense and draining places that exist in the world. Mad sights and sounds unfold around you everywhere, all the time, a relentless fountainhead of overwhelming experience. It is filthy, absolutely filthy, and whether it is an immune response or only a psychological one, somehow constant vigilance against contagion really wears on you. The pollution grates, too, making you cough, making your head ache, your eyes burn. And notwithstanding anything positive you may see atop a pile of trash, the overwhelming sadness of the city tears you down to an extent that is hard to believe. It grinds like a rasp against the very grain of your soul.

We all know that places like Calcutta exist, but to see it—and more than that, to stay immersed in it, to walk the streets for days on end—undermines any illusions one may harbor about order, justice, equality—in a way that is truly world-view shattering.

And so we come at last to my confession. For if nothing else, I must tell you the truth: I was ready to leave Calcutta.

Bangalore

The Way to Bangalore
January 2, 2005

When the time came for me to leave Calcutta, I was still intensely ill. I was feverish, extremely nauseous, vomiting intermittently, and sometimes doubling over with the pain of my cramps. Suddenly the yogis—those ponderous appendages who had so weighed me down, denuding me of freedom of independent movement—seemed my only lifeline to the West. Saying goodbye to everyone I knew in the forlorn Calcutta airport felt like jettisoning weight before a long solo mission into outer space. When the goodbyes were over, the number of people I knew on this side of the globe had been whittled to precisely zero. Ill as I already was, the dawning of this realization only made me feel sicker.

With stomach churning, head throbbing and so fatigued I was barely able to shuffle onto the plane, I boarded an aircraft bound for Bangalore.

I fell into my seat and scanned the motley passengers around me. I didn't expect to feel it, but there it was: a little bolt of fear. *Now you've done it,* that craven voice inside me railed, *you're all alone in India.*

I closed my eyes. Still I saw only trash piles, people crawling in trash; it seemed I could literally smell the trash rotting.

I brought my mind back to the plane, but fared no better. To my immediate left was a man with a species of respiratory ailment that caused him to cough almost constantly. I have never heard anyone hack so long with such intensity. No more than a second or two separated his spasms of coughing, and each blasted exhalation made me want to protect myself from whatever he was spewing into the common air. He hacked incessantly until we landed hours later, and even sprayed a little spittle on my arm. I hated it, of course.

To my right, just across the aisle, was a

shrieking child. He thrashed with an almost maniacal rage, his screams raw and birdlike. This brought the disapproval of every passenger within the range of my vision, but to no avail; the child kept on screaming for more than an hour.

To make matters worse, the airplane was extremely cold. In fact, I haven't been warm in days. Perhaps because it is so damnably hot here in the summers, none of the hotels in India have heaters; instead, they are possessed of arctic, compulsory air conditioning. And there are no blankets. My throat is often sore when I awaken.

Suffice it to say that as ill as I was, I liked neither Coughing Man, Screaming Child, the frigid air, nor the images of stench and garbage squirming like an eel inside me, omnipresent whenever I closed my eyes.

But there I was. As everyone knows, an airplane is not something you can get off of. I thought about my stronger brethren in Calcutta, and tried to meditate, lapsing at last into a fitful sleep.

It was like falling into a well. I was gone. If

someone had wanted to rifle my pockets, pilfer my passport and steal all the remaining cash in my possession, I would have been powerless to stop them. Yet even in sleep I wrestled with something. There was no mistaking it; this was a labored, argumentative slumber. Lifeless as I was, I stayed somehow aware of a madness writhing angrily within me. I was doing battle with it.

When I awoke two hours hence, it was extremely hot; sweat was running down my ribcage and pooling in my belly button. It was so hot, in fact, that my first thought was that I had developed a fever. Then I looked over at Coughing Man. He too was soaking wet—and still hacking away.

We touched down smoothly in Bangalore. I was greeted by a friendly little man who claimed to be the driver for the hotel where I would be staying. His tiny fingers held a sign with my name on it, more or less: ABNERSON. I followed him.

When I stepped into the Bangalore night, staggering along behind my quick-legged driver,

I knew at once that I had landed in another world. The air was so *clean!* I drew the deepest breath I could, a first step to cleansing my lungs. And it occurred to me that I was still alive.

I cannot describe the next events without shame. This is not because I did anything we ordinarily think of as wrong, but because the oasis of cleanliness which awaited me at the Hotel Oberoi was a kind of soft cocoon to which my broken spirit would retreat to mend. I needed desperately to heal myself, to reattach synaptic connections that had been torn asunder—even if in new ways. But why did I require the luxuries of fresh linens and a hot shower to feel safe and whole again, when the whole world slept on the streets?

I was as startled as could be when the driver handed me a bottle of chilled water. It was like heroin to me, like handing a brimming, icy glass to a man who had just staggered, bearded and burned, out of the desert: you knew he needed it, and making sure he got it somehow tacitly acknowledged all he had been through. I sucked its contents down.

We sped away through dusty thoroughfares streaked with the colorful neon lights of high technology concerns: Intel, Tata, Infosys, Sify. And when our little comet finally reached the hotel, I was too exhausted to brush my teeth, ask for a blanket or even take off my clothes. I simply fell on the bed in a filthy heap, sinking without a whimper into a garbage-pile of sleep.

Adventures in Silicon
January 3, 2005

I awoke to dyspepsia, both physical and moral. Calcutta was still sucking the life out of me, a black hole of suffering from which it remained impossible to feel confident of escape.

Even now, a day and a thousand miles later, my soul is still mired there, my mind enslaved by all that I have seen. Every time I close my eyes, I still confront their faces: the poorest of the poor, crawling around in trash in search of sustenance, competing with vermin for the tiniest scraps. My nostrils still smell nothing but garbage. My mouth still tastes pollution, and still I hear the voices of the poor. I am not free.

I washed Calcutta off me, and the water ran away the color of mud. I sat quietly in a dark room trying to forget, but there was no escape from the images in my mind. There was no peace.

I am lost
In the gardens of Bangalore Oberoi
So beautiful these flowers, but
Calcutta is all I can see
I cannot smell the honeysuckle;
only rotting trash fills my nose
and the koi pond, waterfall and colorful saris
are mere transparencies
layered over beggars' eyes.

I want to shake it off
The way a dog shakes off water
I tried to scrub it off, black water running away
I'm going to walk it off, sleep it off—
and carry it with me to my grave.

Exhausted and nauseous as I remained, I adhered to plan and hired a car to take me out to ITPL, Bangalore's Silicon Valley. This was reputed to be the new center of gravity for the intellectual capital of our age, and I wanted to see for myself.

The journey took a longish hour. We passed out of Bangalore proper and through the electron cloud of madness which surrounds the city's nucleus. Here were the usual ludicrous sights—sidewalk bathroom breaks, rampant animals, people glad to take possession of the feces of a cow—but I took not a single photograph. It was all so tame compared to Calcutta.

We moved on, entering a broad swath of land where everywhere I looked, the skeletons of giant new buildings were heaving up out of the ground. It was bizarre to come upon such cutting-edge construction in the broader swirl of India's medieval imagery. But there it was again, the last thing in the world you would expect to see: a gleaming jewel of high technology, rising amid wild goats that strolled long roads of dust.

I got out of the car and tried to enter one of

the silver towers, one bearing all the names: IBM, AOL, Agere, Tata, Sify.

I was rebuffed. This was not a tourist attraction, the guard explained; it was a high-security zone at which I had no business. And, by the way, no photographs were permitted.

But I had come a great distance, and I was determined to slip inside the silicon of the system, to take the pulse of this closeted world; this was in fact my only reason for coming to Bangalore.

I walked away from the security post as though planning to return to the car, but instead merged unnoticed with a crowd of passing engineers, following them down a staircase flanked by man-made waterfalls and into the open-air center of the complex. It was beautiful: mirrored spires labeled "Inventor," "Creator" and "Discoverer" arose like monuments to the power of the human mind. They surrounded a central commons, the focus of life in this isolated, hot-house world.

I happened to be there just at lunchtime, and when the denizens of the crystalline skyscrapers of ITPL streamed forth from their buildings, it was something to see. They were young—their average age was probably twenty-five—and more than half were women. They wore the customary colorful saris; but they were dreaming, I knew, of abstract mathematics.

I moved inside the commons unnoticed. It was a scene so Western that I might as well have been in California. Here was a Pizza Hut, a Kentucky Fried Chicken, and a stereo playing "Every Breath You Take" by Sting. The engineers poured forth *en masse* and ordered lunch in lines akin to Western fast-food restaurants, eating their pizzas casually, as though this were a daily occurrence—which it probably was. I sat nearby and ate one too, without garnering the least bit of attention. I had finally found a corner of India in which I was all but invisible.

The conversation near me, much of it in English, quickly turned to chip sets and algorithms. Voices rose and hands gesticulated eagerly; these were people who discussed microprocessors and their attendant instructions with an ardor we might reserve for heartfelt expressions of romantic love.

They were that rare breed of human being able to interface directly with machines, and as such the most important drones of our time. They walked around with complex segments of computer code, the DNA of an invisible global system, stored inside their minds; they intuited its contours, shaped and sculpted it. And yet they also were its hosts: like disembodied parasites, the strands of code morphed and replicated within them. The engineers' thoughts were but viral obligates, capable of reproduction only if brought forth into the collective, living code.

Every now and then, I spied an elder with white hair and large, thick glasses. These I imagined were the Architects of this new world, conductors of the young programmers' complex dance.

As I made my way out of the building called "Creator," I saw that the commons beneath it contained some forty storefronts, including a doctor, a barber and a lawyer—one-stop shopping for everything a human being could possibly need. Then it hit me: the Architects had created a system in which none of the worker bees would ever have to leave the hive.

I took the long, straight, dusty road back into Bangalore.

The Oberoi Barber
January 3, 2005

When I arrived at the hotel, I decided it was time to peel off another layer of Calcutta. I asked the local barber to trim my beard.

The Oberoi barber set about his attack on the hairs of my neck with his razor set at a frighteningly acute angle and an energy that reminded me of plier-assisted tooth extraction. I prayed he would not cut my throat.

Meanwhile, in the chair next to mine, another patron was having his head slapped, hard and repeatedly, by his "barber." I wondered if this was a special request, or part of the regular treatment. Given the intensity of the cranial pugilism involved, either possibility seemed equally absurd.

I was lost in these thoughts when it became evident my own barber was about to finish. He had shaved my neck, trimmed my moustache and beard, and begun to wipe off my face with a longhaired brush that smelled strongly of *urine*. Now here is how you can tell I had been to Calcutta: I didn't even flinch. In fact, after he trimmed a few more errant sideburn hairs, I let him do it again. And when it was all over, I now realize, I didn't even think to wash my face.

Kozhikode

The Poetry of the Moment

January 4, 2005

"Who sees me in all things and sees all things in me, for him I am never out of sight and for me, he never disappears."

—Lord Krishna
The Bhagavad Gita, 6:29

This morning my meditation focused on the concept of human fidelity. And it occurred to me: we are all intensely true to that which is truly most important to us. And what is that? Only our *conduct* answers.

☀

"Have a pleasant journey, welcome back," said the Oberoi bellman cheerily as I bundled into a cab bound for the Bangalore airport. It is a mangled expression, but one I have heard so many times in India that I have come to love it.

I boarded the Air India flight and crossed a thousand miles of subcontinent in slumber, awakening only when we descended through chop into Cochin, the heart of the South Indian province of Kerela.

The view outside my window had become decidedly more tropical. The endless deserts of the North had given way to shadowy palm forests cut by slow, dark rivers.

I was standing in line at the pleasant little airport in Cochin, waiting for a ticket to Kozhikode, when I began to pay attention to the smallest things: how a man's inadvertent toe on the baggage scale caused its display to flitter up and down; the breezy wanderings of an ancient fan caressing the humid air, back and forth, forth and back; even more slowly, I sensed the glacial wilting of the yellow flowers in the vase before me, giving scale to time.

I reached the front of the line. A woman took my papers, furled her brow, and said, "uhbuhubhuubu," or words to that effect. I asked the officious-looking man to whom she spoke whether everything was all right; I'm always attentive when someone says something like uhbuhubhuubu whilst examining my passport, especially when I'm seven thousand miles from home.

The man's foot removed, the scale fell to zero; the fan completed its arc; and the officious-looking man assured me that it was—all in the same trice.

In that instant, something was revealed to me: God is the poetry of the moment. There is no separateness. God, all, this moment—we—are one. There is so much to see, if only we will look. And now is all there is. Now is the One True Thing.

She brought her stamp down on my ticket like a hammer, handing it to me with a smile.

I smiled back. It had been another gorgeous span of time in which a plethora of little miracles, and absolutely nothing at all, had happened.

Music
January 4, 2005

God is the poetry of the moment: the clock you find, the ocean-crossing power of a smile. A driving Paris rain so cold it hurts your bones, and all the suns of Kozhikode burning your skin.

And music.

The live performance of music, I now see, takes its captivating force from its ability to hold us in the moment. Live music happens *now*. It does not merely exist, hanging on the wall like a painting; it *unfolds*. Its essence is becoming, not being; it opens like a flower that blooms before our very eyes. In this way it mesmerizes us. And when it is over, it is gone.

In that sense, music is so like life: we must take the joy of music as it happens, or not at all. Whether we listen or perform, we are transported, not away from the authenticity of the moment, but into a kind of trance of becoming. Music urges, no, *requires* us to look upon the constantly unfolding vista of the now. In this way, music consecrates the true nature of existence and affirms its miraculous, blossoming depth—even as it disappears.

Kozhikode Kamikaze
(or: How I Wound Up in Cochin)
January 4, 2005

I landed in Kozhikode, near the southern tip of India, and hired a car to drive me into the jungle. It was extremely humid and deadly hot, but even here the women were wrapped from head to toe in saris; I can't imagine how they stand it.

The serpentine road wound through a shadowy forest where everything seemed lifted from *Apocalypse Now*: palm trees, broad dark rivers, banana farms—and thousands upon thousands of the very, very poor.

A little more than an hour later we rounded a turn and I beheld, the glimmering crests of the Arabian Sea. Here was the recent instrument of one hundred fifty thousand tsunami deaths, sleeping.

Ten minutes later, we arrived at the Taj

Residency Calicut, a self-described "business hotel" and the place I had originally planned to regroup before heading for Sri Lanka and the Maldives.

It was incredibly run-down and filthy. Nevertheless, having traveled a very long way to get here, with hopeful countenance I entered my room. It smelled pungently of mildew and, indeed, an ample beard of fungus flourished in the bathroom sink and at the windowsill. The bedspread was streaked with multicolored stains: brown, orange, rusty-red. It was so dirty I hated to even lay my pack on it.

I inquired about the hotel's business center, so as to post this entry to the Internet, only to learn it had been recently destroyed. When I went down to see for myself, I discovered the business center was completely filled with sand. The clamor of shovels, hammers, saws, staple guns and all the other paraphernalia of construction rang out harshly. The coffee shop was also permanently out of service. Exasperated, I went to explore the bar at poolside. It too was gone.

All had been destroyed by the great wave.

On the elevator ride back to my room, I noticed a girl in what could have been a white nurse's uniform carrying a tray of what looked like pillboxes. Each box bore a name and time of day.

It cannot be, I remember thinking, *that this place doubles as a nursing home!* But it was so. The evidence of this was all around me: elderly denizens doddering up and down the hall in their pajamas, a fouled bed pan leaning in the corner near the stairs. The omnipresent musty scent of urine.

No sooner did this realization dawn than I began to plot my escape.

I shall draw a curtain over the innumerable pathways of exodus I considered in my quest to immediately vacate Kozhikode, for the upshot was this: I bolted from the place without sleeping there a single night, hurtling recklessly away from the hotel in the backseat of an odd three-wheeled conveyance piloted by a pimply-faced teenager, a boy whom I encouraged in his natural tendency to drive at nothing short of an outrageous speed by slapping him on the back, cheering him on and, in the end, paying extra. I had a train to catch, and there was no time to spare. And although I had no idea what awaited me, the very moment I departed the Nursing Home Hotel and burst again into the wilds of India, I felt better.

Free! I ran into the train station soaked with sweat, and quickly bought a ticket for Cochin, sprinting under load to catch a train I had been told would be departing moments hence. The thing was, though, the man who sold me the ticket didn't actually *give* me the ticket—a small but crucial detail—so, carrying my every belonging, I had to sprint back and forth across the bridge above the tracks: up twelve stairs, cross the bridge, down twelve stairs, get the ticket, up twelve stairs. . . Well, you get the idea. And yet, despite all that, I made the train— barely. I was streaked with sweat and gasping for breath. There was not a second to spare.

Or so I thought. The next thing that happened was exactly nothing, which is to say, we sat there on the tracks for close to an hour without so much as turning a wheel.

Still, these were exhilarating moments. My plans, first shredded by the tidal wave that swallowed up Sri Lanka and the Maldives, had been rewritten once again by the hand of fate. Now the die was cast, and I was sitting on a train with hundreds of everyday Indians, heading for a city I had never seen beyond its airport, and without so much as a place to sleep for the night. The umbilical cord of my plans had finally been cut. I was rambling free in India.

It was getting dark, and the train ride was scheduled to take five hours. How it didn't take ten is beyond me. The train was flaccid, and seemed to lack the will to move. I'm sure we could have made the trip in ninety minutes had we just kept going. Instead we crept along by fits and starts, loitering at every neon lamp that cut the jungle night.

I wondered how I would fill so vast a span of time—five full hours—trapped with a horde of southern Indians not of my choosing. It was surprisingly easy: as everywhere along my journey, people were interested in me.

Conversation quickly filled the first two hours.

The next three were a little harder to pass. I wrote this entry, studied the train, read the autobiography of Ghandi. I shifted around, stretched my back, peered into the inky darkness on the other side of the train's barred windows, listening to the clatter of the tracks. I considered the benefits of Jainism.

Still there were hours to go.

The passage of time can be slowed by extrinsic conditions; here this principle was soundly proved. For the minutes ticked away all the more slowly owing to the fact that it was hot, damnably hot, and because, having eaten nothing in the preceding thirty-two hours, I was exceedingly hungry. Everyone knows that in these situations, time slows down.

The not eating, if you must know, was a result of two factors: continued stomach cramps, and not finding anything I wanted to consume. I am now completely tired of Indian food. After weeks of eating nothing but curry, I am ready to live out the rest of my days without another bite of it. Of course I know that a month after I get home, I'll be back to my spice-craving self. But at this point, only bread, yogurt and beer look good to me. And these essentials have been unavailable of late.

India, in short, is a wonderful place to lose weight. First you puke your guts out and, when that's done, your stomach is so raw that you can tolerate only the mildest of foods, which are in short supply.

After many bumpy hours on the train, I made Cochin around midnight, found a hostelry not far from the tracks and went to bed again without a bite.

Cochin

A Flick of the Brush

January 5, 2005

Hunger woke me. My first hope was for an uneventful day, a day of resting. That was precisely how it began.

It started, in fact, by the hotel swimming pool. I had groped my way unknowingly in darkness to a truly wonderful hotel. It was clean, orderly and quiet, a womb of safety. Even a casual remark that the washroom lacked paper towels could start a stampede of people eager to rectify the transgression. I was looking forward to a day relaxing here.

I sat by the pool in dawnlight chewing my fourth crusty roll and vowed to rest, telling myself this would be a day in which absolutely nothing happened; and yet—if you can permit me to use so peculiar a turn of phrase—nothing didn't.

Instead, I was forced to go to the airport.

The reason was this: having abandoned Kozhikode in the mad heat previously described, I could no longer fly from there to Mumbai, so I needed to change my ticket or I would miss my flight home. One thing was certain: failing to catch the flight from Delhi to Paris was not in the plan. So off to the airport I went. It turned out to be the best thing I'd done in days.

It didn't start out that way. My driver, a sullen, quiet type, took me to the place directly and in silence. The lady at Jet Airways smiled, but only weakly, and her bindi could have been the Nicobar Islands in a turbulent sea: it was in pieces. She was efficient, but only in a *here's-your-oatmeal* sort of way. It was all so boring.

Then, with a flick of the brush God paints with, everything changed. I asked the driver if he would mind showing me around a bit, perhaps even going as far as Jew Town, and he abruptly fired to life. It was as though he had been running out of battery power and I had plugged him in. He sat up straight and became as animated as a ventriloquist's doll. From then on it was impossible to shut him up.

Not that I would have wanted to. He was a font of information, a magnum of patience, a superabundance of garrulous fun. Far from being the sourpuss I took him for at first, he turned out to be the kind of man you want to take home with you to America, employ at twice his wage for all his working life, then nurse with loving kindness to the precipice of old age and beyond, making sure his thread is tucked securely back into the web of being. His name was Sanil, and I loved him.

We drove for hours. First he took me into Mattancherry, a part of Jew Town, to see the Paradisi Synagogue, circa 1568. Old buildings being just that, we quickly urged the little car to the brink of the Arabian Sea so he could show me what was really on his mind: the Chinese fishing nets. These were contraptions of almost incredible cunning, extremely effective at ripping the fetal saltwater catfish from the uterus of the sea. I assisted in one such murderous procedure, heaving the ropes that bore the weight of the net, the fish, and the ocean itself, hoisting them all skyward. It was arm-numbingly difficult, the kind of work that would callous one's hands, but not until after weeks of making them bleed.

The Arabian Sea. How beautiful it was! I wanted to stay there forever, to paint it with my words for you until it knelt before my feet, saying *you captured me; give me to whomever you choose.* Instead of that, we entered the cavernous darkness of a local bar, an act which at first seemed an abandonment of broader purpose, but soon became a vista all its own.

It was dark inside. God, it was dark. And it stank. But here was a chance to observe the universal language of maleness, the wordless mantra of men. My eyes adjusted and the darkness developed like a photograph, an image filled with white eyes set in weathered, obsidian faces. I spoke but a single word of Malayalam, *Na-NEE*—which means thank you—and the totality of the English spoken by the patrons of that bar could have been written on the back of a postage stamp. Yet here we were, drinking beer and burping like long-lost brothers, harmonious as an old folk song.

We downed our beers and moved on. Sanil showed me St. Francis Church, where Vasco Da Gamma was buried in 1524 before his body was moved to Portugal.

In fact, he showed me everything. We were out all day. Here at last was the India of which I had dreamed: a clean, uncrowded port for shipping spices and perfumes. We passed traders carefully tallying their day's sales on old adding machines in shadowy rooms stacked floor to ceiling with red chili peppers and tea, the products bound with bamboo ties in packets five and six feet tall. We witnessed the cheerful exodus of hundreds of uniformed schoolchildren freed from their busses at the center of town. There were ancient churches, narrow alleyways mounded with sacks of fragrant turmeric and curry, dilapidated quays jammed with ancient fishing boats that looked like Viking ships, powered solely by oar.

At last the happy streets of Fort Cochin, clean

and inviting, fell before Sanil's wheels and the tyranny of coming night.

I got back to the hotel just in time for a buffet dinner. The soup, labeled "apple and earth," turned out to be an excellent cream of potato; think *pomme de terre*, I suppose. And as I ate, I was treated to a stupefying Hindi version of "Knocking on Heaven's Door."

"Mama put my guns in the ground," the pre-pubescent singer crooned with a heavy Indian accent; *"I can't shoot them anymore."*

This to the accompaniment of a *sitar.*

The strange song trapped within me, I headed to the hotel shop and bought a strand of beads the color of Poseidon, tied them to my wrist, and toddled off to sleep.

Vinaya's Song
January 6, 2005

Another dawn found me at poolside, wondering what to do. *I didn't come to India to sit by a pool,* I was thinking, *with all these pale, bloated tourists.*

I had considered going into the Periyar Tiger Preserve, but this would mean eight hours' costly travel by car, and I had been told confidentially that no one has spotted a tiger there in years. The big cats, it seems, keep to themselves. I can't say I blame them.

Then I had a simple idea that totally changed the day: I asked the man at the front desk for a local map.

What it showed amazed me: I was amid a complex archipelago of islands and peninsulas, with what appeared to be ferries between them. The little world around me was transformed—here was an exploration impossible to resist.

I headed out on foot with map in hand to the northern tip of Willingdon Island, then made west towards the water in search of a boat. I had missed the ferry, and the next one would be several hours hence. But as everywhere in India, interstitial carriers were clamoring to meet my needs. For fifty rupees, which is to say about twenty-five cents, a kindly man rowed me across a vast channel— please linger over the word *row*—and deposited me on the eastern bank of Fort Cochin.

I made my way out of the quays and through a labyrinth of narrow alleys, brushing aside a man who tried to sell me hashish before intersecting with a kind of high street. It was clean, bustling with traders selling spices and perfumes, weighing bundles of tea, making entries in ledgers. Glorious fragrances wafted on a warm sea breeze. Jasmine. Curry. Sandalwood.

I walked on, passing an ancient church, and entered a small shop. Here I encountered a teenaged girl named Vinaya who decided— quite of her own accord, and without any kind of warning—that what I needed most was to hear her sing. In Hindi. For a very long time.

Without a word, she gazed into my face and burst into song.

It would have been impossible not to listen. She sang beautifully, her voice a shimmering wave, and kept it up until I was transfixed, staring into the garden of carved idols behind her.

Shiva, the destroyer. Lakshmi, goddess of wealth. Ganesh, remover of obstacles. Durga, the unconquerable. Vishnu, the preserver.

I wandered the Fort for several hours more to the soundtrack of Vinaya's ancient melody before crossing the long bridge back to Willingdon Island, closing a loop of perhaps twelve miles. The sun was setting now, so I made for the hotel and its inviting pool.

I swam alone in darkness, bathing off the day. Then I sat in an extended meditation. The faces of the idols returned to my mind's eye: Ganesh, the elephant-god. The six arms of Shiva. Saraswati, plucking her sitar.

When I emerged from meditation an hour later, I was thinking: *My learning is very shallow, but I have learned this: I need to learn.*

Vyppen
January 7, 2005

It was dawn again, and hot. A man in a starched white coat brought me some coffee, and I read the paper: AWARENESS CAN REDUCE THE SPREAD OF AIDS, it said. THE NAVY IS HELPING TSUNAMI

VICTIMS. In short, nothing really new.

It felt as though today might be the one day without incident, a day in which the whole world took a breath and simply rested. A day, in short, when nothing much happened. But I knew that it could never be so.

Because although we rarely stop to think about it, on any given day catastrophe strikes. It's scale may be small—a tractor-trailer running over a single child—or vast, as in the recent tsunami. But at any given instant I tell you—hell, *as you are reading these words*—someone in this world of ours is dying, losing a child, undergoing an amputation, being told that he or she has only a week to live. Makes one think about the preciousness of health in the present moment, doesn't it? For these are everyday occurrences on Earth. But when catastrophe doesn't strike us directly, it is often all but invisible. Yet we also know that one day it will be our turn.

Even this fact remains shrouded most of

the time. Like a painting hidden under canvas in the attic, the prospect of an adverse fate is known, yet plausibly denied. "Death comes," as Camus wrote, "but not today."

To those who have dusted off the canvas, though, and hung the painting of death within the very living rooms of their lives, its message is clear: *Live now!* For though the contours of the image in the painting—the time and mode of one's demise—remain obscure, coming into focus only lately if at all, the murky, undeveloped scene within that frame still speaks with a precision and convincing force to put Cicero in envy. Its message is not, "You shall die," but rather, "Now is the time to truly live!"

I issued forth into the day. A long walk would become a mini-marathon, I knew, so I stopped for an inspirational espresso at the Malabar. Here I was surrounded by tourists whose idea of a trip to India consisted of lying around at poolside listening to the stuff stored on their iPods and chattering by cell phone with the folks back home. Why come to India at all? And yet there they lay, blissed out in the deafened isolation of their headphones as I listened to a far-off Muslim prayer song spilling into the sky, exotic and enchanting as a dark-eyed child.

I drank the good espresso and moved on, its energy electrical within me. This was the land of the head shakers, the side-to-side gesture of those who speak Malayalam, and I was eager to get back out there with them.

I walked on to the place where I knew I would find my ferryman, who by now had become my friend. He often waited in a shady spot not far from the Malabar.

We greeted as though we had known each other many years, and I gave him fifty rupees to row me across the channel. That was the standard price he set, the equivalent of a quarter. But when we got to the other side, I gave him fifty more, which made his face shine like the sun, his white teeth bared and glistening. I knew his economics, and I knew mine. It was twenty-five cents so well worth spending, the best two bits I ever handed to a man.

I bailed out of the boat and into the street, turning left to find the perfumier. The day before he had made me a concoction he declared unique in all of India. It might have been, but it wasn't quite right, and today it was pure sandalwood oil I wanted. I got it, but for six dollars, a price that would have paid the boatman's rent for a month.

I made for the northwest perimeter of the Cochin peninsula, and Vyppen Island beyond. Here lay the outer orbit of my trip to India.

I happened to walk up just as the Vyppen ferry was departing, and boarded it by leaping over a cable, the last soul aboard. We heaved out into the strait.

It was a crossing of meridians for me. Here in Vyppen was that outer extremity, that farthest edge of the world, I had wanted in the Maldives; here I was so far from home the tether leading back seemed but a dream.

It was the sort of place my father would have loved: clean, simple, temperate, bounded on all sides by the sea. For Vyppen

is an island, a gem in the archipelago of
Mattancherry, a wanderer's bliss. I sat on the
beach and wrote:

> *Be here now,*
> *in the poetry of the moment*
> *give thanks*
> *for all that you are*
> *give your love*
> *as though today was your last*
> *go slowly,*
> *and notice things.*
>
> *You know the truth:*
> *health is your treasure*
> *You know the truth:*
> *to deserve love*
> *you must give the kind of love you seek.*
>
> *You know the truth:*
> *the less you need*
> *the more your wealth is increased*
> *You know the truth:*
> *you owe it to yourself*
> *to live as you believe.*

I walked the desolate beach at Vyppen all alone,
sensing I was in search of something. Whatever it

was, I didn't find it. I climbed over driftwood, rummaged in jetsam, pondered the sky; but nothing. It was not to be. This beach had given nothing to me.

Or had it? In town again, I bought an orange and sucked down its essence. The bright day caressed my skin. I thought about my father, how he would have looked in a longhi. It was easy to see him like that. It was the way he should have always dressed. He never did.

Things moved and changed inside my mind; ambiguous shapes emerged from the murky limbo, then quickly rearranged themselves again. It was like an alien child playing around with Lego blocks in there. My conscience seemed to have sprouted a will of its own. A kite, freed of its tether. A horse, sensing the absence of bridle and rein. I decided to just let it go—or maybe it was letting go of *me*.

We walked on, my mind and I, ignoring each other, until some children on a bus called out to us. This was a jolt. My mind was a piece of See's candy flopping backwards into its mold. We were awake, alert, reunited, aware of the gentle ocean breeze.

The ferry came again, and I took the vessel back to Fort Cochin in silence.

Lost
January 8, 2005

We have, in the end, to trust in something beyond reason, whether it be love, God, or simply ourselves. In addition to the many advantages accorded to a Westerner by right of birth, I have been lucky to possess one sentinel edge: in my own mind, at least, I always enjoy the benefit of the doubt.

Days came and went, relentless. Places merged together like the colors of the sunrise on the palette of my mind. I walked alone on seashores without hurry, merging with the ocean's invisible breeze. I spanned the nameless places between islands in a listless dinghy, drunk on warm air and the endless superabundance of time. I was lost.

The Boatman's Tale
January 8, 2005

This evening found me wandering along the northern shore towards the naval yard; here I came to a beach that had been ravaged by the recent tidal wave. But hidden among the dunes, careless of the fact of the tsunami, were lovers, kissing in the shadows, showing how life goes on. They made me glad and sick at the same time.

I made for the farthest edge of the peninsula; the distances were very great. As I passed by the naval yard, I came upon ever-more friendly people, until I was literally mobbed.

What wonderful people, I remember thinking, *who live in this wonderful place.* And the way their heads wag side-to-side when they smile—I tell you, if the whole world would but adopt this single custom, it would mean an end to wars.

It was late, time to eat, and my throat was dry for a beer. I had walked and walked and walked, and now I wanted my boatman. I wasn't sure where to find him, so I wandered down to the quays to look around. There he was, as though he had been waiting for me all the day. And indeed, he might have been. This was India, after all, and I was his customer.

I sent him into the town on a borrowed bicycle to purchase two beers: one for him and one for me. This he did with pure honor, bringing the beer and more change than he promised from the money I had given him.

We rowed out, and but for one another we were totally alone. It was the simplest of things: two men in a rowboat on a quiet sea. When we got to the middle of the waterway, he put down his oars. We drank and talked about our lives. There were so many ways we overlapped: the people we loved, the kinds of things that worried us. Our rowboat flowered to a Venn diagram with a vast, dark center. A long silence settled in.

"I want to tell you a story," he began.

"It was the time of the monsoon, and a terrible storm battered all of Kerela. A rich spice trader lay awake in his bed, his beautiful wife in his arms, their three small children gathered around them. They were listening to the rain.

"Suddenly a massive flood burst through the walls, and they were swept away in all directions, screaming, powerless to resist. He never saw his family again.

"The man was fortunate. He was very strong, and lashed himself to a spar of wood. It is a miracle he was not eaten by the sharks. But he survived.

"Four nights later he washed up on the southern shore of Fort Cochin with nothing but the clothes on his back.

"His family and all of his possessions had been destroyed. People knew about his unfortunate circumstances. One townsman gave him a tin bowl, and another gave a sleeping mat. He began the life of a beggar.

"As he regained his strength, the townspeople noticed that he had a knack for storytelling. He could really weave a tale—"

Here the boatman paused for a long pull on his beer.

"The children loved his stories most. They followed him wherever he went. He told them the stories he had told his own children: fables, things like that. Old stories. But he gave the old stories new life.

"He told the story of two elephants, one called Little Neelandan and the other Parkutty, Neelandan the rowdier of the two. Have you heard that fable?"

I had not.

"There was a local farmer named Kuttiali who had heaped up a mountain of cow manure for fertilizer near the river. Two men, Thoma and Raman, set out to pilfer a canoe of it.

"The plan was to steal the dung at midnight when most of the villagers were asleep. There happened to be no moon. The thieves paddled along the dark, flooded river, navigating her hidden undercurrents. Then they climbed out to steal the dung.

"It was a huge black heap. One of the thieves, Raman, cut into the pile with his shovel. But the heap of dung was actually an elephant, sleeping. Little Neelandan, no less. She roared. Dogs barked! The village woke up.

"The thieves jumped into the river. Days later they were found, five miles downstream.

Raman was hiding in the top of a tree, still so frightened he would only call out like an owl.

"Then there was the story about how the same foolish men tried to steal Parkutty, the gentler elephant. Think of it: trying to steal an elephant! What kind of fool would attempt such a thing? But the world is full of fools. Of that you can be certain, Joseph.

"The thieves spent weeks in preparation. Elephant theft, they reasoned, was a difficult business. It required much more cunning than stealing money, gold or jewels, or even women.

"Although the elephant was held only by a small leg-tether, the severing of that tether by one whose body odor was unfamiliar to the beast could lead to disaster: the elephant might smash him into the ground.

"Thoma and Raman, the fools, believed that they had found a better way. They obtained a stalk of fragrant, ripe bananas. Soon the elephant thieves were courting Parkutty every night with stalks of banana and jaggery balls, trying to win her favor and make her familiar with their scents.

"At last the night came. It was overcast, and a light rain fell. It seemed the whole village was asleep; no light filtered out of the homes.

"One of the thieves stood in front of the elephant with a stalk of banana, and the other unbuckled the chain. But the dark mass burst up, not into a tame walk but into an arrogant gait. It wasn't Parkutty, the gentle elephant; it was Little Neelandan! The one with the angry, bloodshot eyes. The ruthless one!

"Things done in darkness are often mistaken. It is wise to remember that.

"So and so," said the boatman, smiling broadly and shaking his head from side to side, "the widowed spice trader told the ancient fables to the children of the town."

Then he paused. Reflecting.

"He was a smart man. At a time when there was record unemployment in the town, he, a mere beggar, managed to obtain a job. He worked in a spice dock, loading and unloading sacks until his muscles rippled like those of a much younger man.

"He saved his earnings, too, living simply. Ten years later he had enough saved to open his own importing company. He was a wealthy spice trader once again.

"He bought a big house on the west side of Cochin and furnished it with things to remind him of his past: sandalwood carvings and silks of the kind that had adorned his former home. But he was restless in these surroundings, tossing and turning in his big white bed.

"He used to sneak out of the house at night and sleep on the ground. He had kept the bent tin bowl and dirty sleeping mat as mementoes of his years as a beggar, and he would take these with him.

"This happened more and more frequently, until his habit was discovered.

"The townspeople thought he was insane. 'You are a rich man; go back into your house,' they would say; but he would not go back. He would cling to his bent tin bowl and ask them for an offering as though his life depended on what they might give.

"During the day, he ignored his trading company and went instead to that place near the center of the town where the children come pouring out of their busses after school. And again the children gathered around him, still eager to hear his stories. He told them how Vishnu created Fort Cochin, and all of Kerela, by hurtling his axe into the Earth near the edge of the sea, splitting the land into islands. Without this act by Vishnu, there could never be boatmen like me! And he told the fables of the elephant thieves...

"He never did return to his house. He let it fall apart. His trading company, too, shut down, and was declared in bankruptcy. They say he didn't even show up at the court. It was right over there—"

Here the boatman paused, interrupting his story a third time, and turned to point towards an area of gutted warehouses at the curve of the horizon. "You can almost see it from here.

"For forty years he has lived among us, weaving his stories and teaching the children. He has remained penniless but always possessed of a smile."

"I would like to meet this man," I said. "Can we do that tomorrow?"

"No," he said, without a hint of emotion. "He has just been drowned in the tidal wave, a second time swept away into the sea."

The tidal wave. I hadn't thought about it much in days. As I wandered the Cochin archipelago, thousands of bodies were burning in massive, anonymous pyres. How close I had come to being one of them. If I had flown to Malé ten days earlier than planned...

The boatman moved his shoulders in a way that let me know his story was over, then quietly picked up his oars. The sea lapped at the prow; the oarlocks groaned, the binding of wet rope against wood. The sun was setting now, and we rowed forward, towards what remained of our lives.

Gradually the gemstones of the sea were taken down; I watched it happen as he rowed. And when we reached the other side, and I alighted there, he paddled into the darkness with a liquid, wooden sound, and I walked away, knowing I would never see him again.

Last Day in India
January 9, 2005

My last day in India began in mundane fashion, with packing and a shower. I washed my whole body with special care, anointed it with essences of lime and sandalwood purchased in Cochin, and donned a cotton Indian shirt. I was starting to say good-bye.

The boy at the restaurant pointed it out, with more than a little envy: I would have lunch in Cochin, tea in Bombay, dinner in Delhi and breakfast in Paris. How many people, he wondered aloud, can ever hope to live like that?

We lifted out of Cochin gently, flying north across Mangalore, Udipi, Panaji. We passed many places I would love to have visited—Mysore, Pune, Goa—but India is vast, far too vast to explore in a month. Then we descended into the rusty hills around Bombay.

I changed planes and plied northward, crossing the Gulf of Khambhat before passing Ahmadabad, Kota and Jaipur. Night fell along the journey; the darkness outside my window was totally unbroken as we crossed the barren Aravalli Range. Then, out of nowhere, came the lights of Delhi.

I deplaned and was shocked by what I saw: it was a spotless modern airport, nothing like the hovel I had written of a month before. Had fairies descended on the place and cleaned it? Or had the whole thing been destroyed and then rebuilt anew? No, it was *my eyes* that had changed, and what had seemed so filthy as I entered India now appeared as spotless as an altar. The Delhi airport was the cleanest place I had seen in a month. I would have eaten off its floor.

And wow, was it bustling. People were moving around quickly, way too quickly for me. My baggage came almost before I was ready for it, almost annoyingly soon. It had not seemed that way before. In India, I realized, I had slowed down.

I took a cab into Delhi, back to the hotel where it had all begun. Along the way my driver got lost, utterly lost, in a dark and crowded slum, but I didn't panic; my experience with Indian people and the situations that commonly arise here was such that I didn't so much as uncap a pen.

Down at the hotel bar an hour later, an older German man and I got talking. Through the acrid cloud of smoke arising from his black-tar European cigarette, he explained that he had recently traveled to Siberia. Interested, I asked him how it was. His answer revealed the mechanics of his soul: "It was spectacular," he said, a distance in his eyes; "but unimportant."

The conversation fell over like a dead tree.

The waiter and I, though, spoke of many things: death, love, India, crossing the ocean. In the end Majid Farooq, as he was called, threw up his hands. "Man proposes," he said, bringing forth the worn adage, "but God disposes." It was true, so very true. I finished my beer and left.

As I was walking out, a tarot reader grabbed my arm, looked me square in the face and said quite earnestly that I was her soul-mate. She *begged* me to go with her, *right now,* to meet her father, who, it seemed, was quite nearby... But I, of course, declined. Who can catalogue the manifold entreaties, the million little dangers that await the weary traveler in India? I returned to the airport.

We achieved lift-off around 2:00 a.m. I tell you when the wheels left the ground, and I was no longer in any sense in India, I felt a pang. For I have grown to love India, the middle, the South and the North. The craziness, the intensity. But most of all, the warmth and kindness of the Indian people.

I forced my mind ahead. To be sure, there were things to look forward to in Europe. Wine and coffee, for example. To say nothing of cheese.

It was with these thoughts nestled like babes in the womb of my mind that the night became sleep; and sleep, thank God, became dreams.

Paris

Pre-Dawn in Paris
January 9, 2005

I fell asleep in the East and awoke in the West, dreaming away the distance between the first and third worlds.

We landed in Paris at 5:28 a.m. local time and were greeted by total darkness. In Cochin the shops would just be opening. There it was almost 10:00.

I knew it would be cold in Paris, the Internet had told me so. Still I was not prepared for the arctic blast that awaited me. Parisians lolled about in parkas that made them look like Eskimos, as though they expected and perhaps even enjoyed this sort of thing. I shivered and pulled on my gloves.

The airport was dim and deserted. I found

the baggage claim and waited for my backpack to appear among the luggage circling on the carousel. Time slithered by; the other passengers claimed their bags and left. I found myself alone in half-light, staring at the forlorn, tattered baggage no one claimed. It was stuck in a weird perpetual orbit, going around and around. What would it take to free it from this destiny, I wondered? What had its intended harbor been? I was lost in thoughts like these when reality set in: still my backpack, container of my every possession, had not appeared. And it never would.

The reason was this: I was standing at the wrong carousel. While the more sensate members of my species were happily plucking their bags and springing forth into the icy darkness of the Paris morn, I was staring mindlessly at intercontinental detritus, musing about its significance in the scheme of things, its place in the universe, its fate.

I began to hunger. During my long hibernation *en route*, a dinner had been served (three courses no doubt, knowing those irrepressible gourmands at Air France), a movie shown, and breakfast furnished with the subdued fanfare only agents of Air France can achieve. But you could prove none of this by me. I had curled up, snuffled and drooled away the entire flight, and the robotic dance of the white-coated stewardesses was less than a dream, merely a creature of imagination, to me. As a consequence, I was extremely hungry.

The airport was forlorn, the café closed. But I could see inside, through the metal bars lowered across the storefront. And Lord, I could smell the croissants—*croissants*, mind you— baking just a few yards away. Even from this distance, and through the sweaty window of the glass oven, I could see them slowly rising. I imagined their buttery, crusty texture in my chompers.

Three dastardly bakers were enjoying their espressos at the counter; they showed not a hint of desire to open the café to me. Instead, they seemed almost gleeful to be closed. But they had to open up eventually. And I was a desperate man. I could wait.

I did just that, and as the minutes ticked by it occurred to me that an adventure in Western cuisine would require money. It was then that I discovered the *bureau de change* was closed: this was an eventuality for which I was unprepared. I slung my heavy pack to the floor and rifled its contents. Could it harbor enough Euros? It could. Thirty-two of them, to be exact. I was rich! Eight would be required for the bus ride into Paris, but the others were mine to do with as I pleased. Suddenly, as if on cue from God above, the café screen heaved open and I rushed inside, Euros in my palm and tongue watering.

I don't know whether it was only the fact that I hadn't had a decent cup of coffee in almost a month, or something deeper. But these synchronous events—the Swiss Family Robinson-esque discovery of so many Euros in my backpack, and the sudden opening of the café—produced in me an exaggerated response bordering on ecstasy. An almost religious degree of appreciation rose up deep within me. I quaffed a large, strong coffee, and gratefully mauled the freshest croissant I have ever eaten. Then I walked to the perimeter of the airport, braced myself, and stepped into the cold.

I took a Roissybus to the Paris Opera House, watching it all glide by: the sterile, empty streets devoid of living things. No dogs, cows or people moved amid the steel and concrete. I saw the Gucci signs, and the Omega; there was the Ferragamo this and the Bruni that. And Karl Lagerfeld, always preposterous among them. *What do we get*, I remember thinking, *from wearing a shirt that costs more than the boatman's family needs to live for a year? Is it not criminal to want such a thing?*

I walked the streets, rush hour blossoming around me, and saw Paris through the eyes of an alien. It is strange indeed to come in a day from the south of India, with its sunny climate and friendly people, to winter in Paris. In fact, it is nothing short of an object lesson in the value of love.

So much is lacking in Paris: it is so bleak, clean, barren, dead and aseptic; there are so few people; and there are no animals to speak of. But here is the real heart of it: when the people do come out, hurrying here and there, nobody smiles. In India my smile said I knew the secret of the whole world, and in a manner of speaking, I did, for my smile was always returned. A smile was a key that opened up the universe.

Here in Paris, no one smiles at me, and to tell you the truth, it makes me sad. *How can it be?* I kept thinking. *This is the so-called "civilized" world.*

But when I smile at people here, they look at me with a mixture of disdain and mild fear. It's very disconcerting. And here's the sad part: to get along in Paris, I stopped smiling.

Silvered
January 9, 2005

I spent the whole day walking alone in Paris. The first task was to find the Bikram Yoga Studio, the place where I would heal myself from all that I had seen and endured. I headed north, via Rue de La Paix, turning left on Avenue d'Opera. Here I was accosted by an elderly, hunchbacked beggar.

The woman *moaned*—literally moaned out loud—and I gave her a few coins. Suddenly the sun broke free of the clouds and gold flared up in the rightmost corner of my peripheral vision. A ray of naked sunlight had struck the godlike pediment of the Paris Opera House, setting fire to the perfect beings exalted there. The meaning of it all was obvious, and you needn't have been to India to see it. Here again screamed the chasm between the weak and the powerful, the decrepit and the healthy, the outcast and the sanctified. It was everywhere, I knew, and always would be.

I moved on, skirting behind the Opera House and turning right on Haussmann. After an hour's hike I came within sight of La Sacré Coeur, then found Rue Faubourg, which on maps is shown, perturbingly, as Rue de Montmartre. There, at Number 17, I found the yoga studio. No sign, nothing to mark the place. Just a button to push. I would push it tomorrow.

I moved on, north to La Fayette, where I ate a pizza. This, you must believe, was a delicacy almost beyond comprehension after several weeks in India. It was covered with fresh mushrooms, garlic, and mounds of French cheese. My regard for it bordered on, no *was*, raw lust. And I was saddened when, in what seemed like an instant, it was gone.

Another hour, a few more miles, another coffee. I turned right on Boulevard de Magenta, making the long, hard slog down to Place de Republique in a light rain. There among the drunks that inhabit the place, I re-oriented myself to the map, then set out via Avenue de la Republique for La Cimitière du Père Lachaise.

For me, no trip to Paris is complete without a pilgrimage to Chopin's grave; his waltzes are what I listen to when life starts spiraling out of control, and they have reeled me in on more than one occasion.

It was a glorious day to walk alive among the dead, the light silvered by the thinnest layer of high-flung clouds. Clouds that seemed to rue their icy altitude, as though some jealous god had cast them there with malice, to keep them far from joy. And I returned, for the first time since my earliest trip to Paris, to Jim Morrison's grave. I had been alone then, too, twenty-one years old and utterly in awe; beautifully, I was no less so now.

It was time to move on, and I did, albeit in the wrong direction. My intent was to exit at Rue de la Rouquette, which I managed, and to turn right on Boulevard Voltaire, heading through a series of carefully scripted turns to Musée Picasso. But instead I turned left—who can say why?—and wandered for a long time before staggering into Place de la Nation in an icy drizzle, cold, tired and lost. Jetlag had my foot in its mouth. I thought about going down to the river, but knew that the only thing left for me to do today—the only thing of which I was really capable—was to go home. So I tucked myself into a far-flung outlet of the Paris metro and emerged near Montmartre. There I bought a bottle of good red wine, a warm baguette, and a hunk of cheese. And that, to say the truth, is all I know; the rest is lost to me.

Paris, Yoga, Louvre
January 10, 2005

My second day in Paris dawned, annoyingly, at

5:00 a.m. It was the time change, working its toll; for according to my body it was already nine o'clock, well past the time to get up. I tried to sleep longer, but there was nothing for it; like it or not, as Lazarus, I was risen.

I puttered about, hoping for coffee, but none could be procured. I was told it was just too early. Of course the truth is otherwise; it is never too early for coffee. But try to convince the guys in room service of that. I had stopped trying.

A map of the city became the object of my fascination, and I studied it the way a teenaged male might examine a centerfold.

Dawn came at last, brutally bright, stark and cold. I ate a bit too much—I had eaten lightly the night before—and blearily walked the path to the yoga room.

The studio was capacious. A pale beam poured in through a huge skylight, casting the floor in a comforting glow. I smiled, bought a four-day pass, and stepped inside.

A photographer was setting up a large, expensive-looking camera, and I learned that he would be capturing the rigors of our session for

Le Monde. Excitement filled the studio.

The class began. At first it didn't seem hot, and I felt terrific. After being crammed into so many cabs, trains and airplanes, it was wonderful to stretch.

It took me awhile to realize what was happening, but twenty minutes into the practice, I was dying. The instructor held us in *ardha chandrasana*, the half moon posture, for what felt like, and must in fact have been, three full minutes per side. This did not alarm me at first. But while we waited to come out of the pose, my mind wandered in non-yogic fashion. *Where will she make up the time?* I mused, *or is this to be a two-and-a-half-hour practice?*

Soon I got my answer. Her proposition, impossible to resist by virtue of the fact that she was the instructor, was to delete all rest between the standing postures.

This was a murderous decision. The heaters were pumping, the room now a hundred and five degrees. All around me, yogis lean as Gandhi were dropping to their knees without a hint of shame. Some even tried to leave the room. (That is not generally permitted.) Everywhere I looked was bliss or mortal pain: bliss on the faces of those who could hang on, pain for those who had learned they could not. I was still standing.

But I was shattered. Then it hit me: I was still working out the poisons of Calcutta. I said a silent prayer to all the souls I left behind and leaned with renewed determination into *tuladandasana*, the balancing stick pose, as the instructor counted 10, 9, 8...

At last we dropped to the floor, and the burden of gravity was lifted. But the spine strengthening series, as it is called, is the toughest part of the practice, and by the time the class was over, it was all I could do to regain control of my breath.

I sat panting in the men's dressing area for twenty minutes, sweat pouring out of me. I still wasn't ready to move. I bought a water from the front desk and watched in awe as the Parisian women with whom I had just practiced issued forth in fancy dresses and high heels, their ample manes already blown dry. Half an hour before, they were trembling with exhaustion and leaking sweat; now they could have peopled the pages of *Vogue.*

Eventually, I found the strength to shower and get dressed, and slipped into the bright morning feeling brand new. My face glowed with a pinkness it had not possessed since Agra. I was coming back to life.

I made south for the Seine and entered the Louvre. I know my way around inside the great museum; still, seeing what I came to see took several hours.

I began with a plan to omit the sub-ground floor and move directly to the ancient Greek sculptures; this I still believe to have been a good decision. For the day was clear, the light unbroken by cloud, and the marbles were cast in deepest definition by mere hazard of the weather.

I was enthralled. You know it when you see the *Venus de Milo*, that magisterial symbol of the absurd, in the glow of a winter sun. You know it when Canova's *Psyche and Cupid* stands against the daylight like a moon.

The long hall of Italian drawings brimmed with

the usual religious art that fills museums the world over nowadays; the only exception was the *Mona Lisa,* drawing her insipid, flash-bulb popping crowds. She smiled coyly from behind glass, but didn't capture me.

Then I tumbled to the Winged Victory, *Nike of Samythrace*, queen of my heart. What could be more beautiful? The Taj Mahal must shake at the comparison.

And that was only the beginning.

I was enslaved by *Le Jeune Martyre*, dealing with the death of a young woman, in much the way I had been stunned by the painting of Lady Jane Grey—shown about to be beheaded—on my way through London weeks before. I was fascinated to learn that both paintings were wrought by the same hand.

I moved upstairs, taking in two Canalettos that were nothing as fine as those I had seen in London, and finding the Vermeers locked away for restoration. Locked away! Just as they had been the last time I was here. They have been shuttered now for close to three years. When will I ever see them?

Eventually, I left the Louvre and changed hotels,

moving up into Montmartre, nearer the yoga studio.
and bedded down for the night.

Napoleon, Orsay
January 11, 2005

Walking in Paris
you do not meet my eyes
and I am nothing more to you
than driftwood passing by.

Walking in Paris this morning, I was arrested yet
again by the harsh sterility of a major Western city.
Paris is a place where people would rather blather
into their cell phones than as much as acknowledge
your existence. In India I was greeted ten times a
minute; here I am lucky if anyone acknowledges
me once in two days. If not their cell phones, then
their headphones shutter them away. Are their
iPods pouring forth the essence of authentic being
into their ears?

With time and new perspective, I began to
see quite clearly that India, with all its

challenges, was the best place I have ever been.

I made the thirty steps or so from my hotel room to the yoga class. It was all different today: I was terribly strong. It was as though I had found my way at last to my native planet, a place where the very atmosphere empowered me.

After yoga, I showered and climbed the many steps to Sacré Coeur, then made left along the ridgeline, descending in due time towards the river. It was a cold, blustery, overcast day, and the windy rain slowed my progress.

At last I passed the several miles that lay between Montmartre and Napolean's tomb, paid a fee, and entered the Hôtel des Invalides, France's national war museum and the resting place of Monsieur Bonaparte.

It didn't do much for me. Here was a place dedicated to the celebration of persons whose sole distinction was their capacity for mass killing. It was a celebration of slaughter, a museum in which a very small man lay housed within a ludicrously oversized tomb. It was, in addition, poorly organized, barely curated and partially under construction. As a kind of protest, I limited my photographs to three.

I moved on, walking south along Rue des Invalides, away from the Seine. The sky angered and spat a cold rain. I was moving towards Musée Rodin, alive as all get-out, but thinking about death. *The Shah Jahans of the world, and the Napoleans, may be entombed within the walls of little man-made heavens,* I reflected, *as close to immortality as can, by humans, be attained. But they are just as dead.*

All is in flux. The world that greets my eye does not consist of being, but *becoming.* Change is happening around us, in every single particular thing, but it is often so incremental as to go unnoticed—especially if we are tempted by denial. And yet, walking alone today, I saw the sidewalks cracking underfoot, the trees abruptly shooting forth the leaves of spring, and children growing old before my eyes. All was a metamorphosis in progress, a slow devolution to entropy, and it could not be denied.

There were no exceptions. I knew that even within the opulence of a crypt that cost enough to feed a million Calcuttans their entire lives, the same rules applied. Instinct told me that deep inside that massive sarcophagus, the withered remains of Napoleon, brittle as an untanned bearskin, yielded to gravity from time to time. It was happening slowly, but it was happening nonetheless: pieces of him were breaking off and going to ground. Even his coffin was shedding a molecule here, a molecule there. That is the way of things, and always will be.

I moved on, north towards the rain-gray river. Here, for the first time, I explored Musée d'Orsay. It was a glory, and I will return again and again.

I started with Stieglitz. I have never been an aficionado of museum-quality photography. Paintings and sculpture are much more accessible to me. But this time it was different.

I had taken over a thousand photographs in the preceding four weeks. Suddenly, Stieglitz's work truly came to life for me.

I observed in him two principle gifts: a brilliant eye for composition and a playful use of focus, that is, where he puts the sharpest edge of his lens. *City of Ambition* exemplifies both: here he composes using vertical lines, and the steam-exuding buildings seem the subject. But a close examination of the photograph reveals that they are slightly out of focus, and the focal subject matter of the work is but a splash of white light in the foreground, glimmering atop a wavelet in the river. Delicious.

I moved on, into a collection almost without peer. Great works of cubism, including paintings by Georges Braque and Max Weber, were everywhere, as were large collections of Pissarro, Cézanne and Degas. And I beheld, for the first time outside the pages of an art history book, *Whistler's Mother*.

Then I rounded a corner and discovered, with a gasp—for I had not carefully read the plan of the museum—a room filled with Van Goghs.

Three paintings stood above the rest. The first, *La Nuit Etoilée, Arles*, seemed almost a study for *Starry Night*. The other two were self-portraits.

The first of these, from 1887, conveyed without a word the artist's tortured, syphilitic mind. The other, *Portrait de l' Artiste, 1889*, was for me an evocation of ever-transient becoming, the artist seeming to melt into the writhing, blue background, himself composed of elemental writhing blue.

I left the museum and moved away in darkness, proceeding east along the left bank of the Seine, and crossed at Pont Royal, the black river topped by colored wavelets of artificial light.

I had to get home. I had practiced yoga, toured two museums and walked for more than seven hours. There was work to be done. It was time to sit down and write about it.

Yoga and My Man Picasso
January 12, 2005

The dominatrix was back in yoga class today, the one who cranks the heat too high, holds the postures too long and skips all the rests in between. Surely she is a disciple not merely of Monsieur Bikram, but of Marquis de Sade. When the class was over, I barely had the energy to pull on my pants.

And I have miles to go, the saying goes, *before I sleep;* for today is to mark my maiden voyage to Musée Picasso, followed by a very long walk along *rive gauche*, the left bank of the Seine.

I reached the museum in the early afternoon; with Paris under sunny skies, the galleries were flooded with warm, yellow light. It is an elegant, if small museum, embued with a humble intimacy. I passed several grateful hours there.

I was struck that Picasso's work is uniformly not so much moving as it is full of mirth, not so much powerful as playful. And irreverent: there were many examples in which he simply let the paint run down. What most would call error, he dared to call a fact of life, no, part of a masterpiece. I loved it!

Several works in the collection hit my core: there was Cézanne's *Château Noir*, now among my very favorite paintings. But the one that really stole my heart was Picasso's *Femme Nue Allongee*. What a silly, gorgeous thing it was. I took it in with lonely joy, then wandered back to the street.

I made south, turning right on Beaumarchais, and looked at the map just in time to turn as planned onto Henry IV, heading back down towards the Seine.

I crossed the river, wandered along the cold left bank and due west on Port de la Tournelle; it was an icy, crystalline day. Soon I came to Pont de Lánchevêde, and the precipice of Cathédrale Notre Dame.

The Thing About My Dad
January 12, 2005

I came at last to Pont Double and turned right, heading due north. For the first time in my life I entered the Cathedral at Notre Dame. I was moved; no, I was all but baptized. I walked as though I were a bishop to the very front of the place, then noticed I had dropped to my knees. I didn't care who saw me, or what they thought. I was thanking God for all my glories—the chances I have had and taken, the love that I have given and received—when suddenly it hit me: I had not forgiven myself for my father's death.

I exhale. This is difficult to admit, and even harder to write: I failed him.

My father was a truly great man. He was a life-long student, a teacher, a tremendous giver of love, and a philosopher. He taught me how we live solely by the consent of those around us, and how that consent can never be taken for granted. He taught me courage by example, and showed through action how skills are earned, not born. There were so many things he taught me— things that were and shall remain our secrets— that I could fill a book with them. He was my hero, my Odysseus, the North Star in my sky. How harsh a fate it is to fail him.

After he fell and hit his head, his speech began to slur. I should have boarded a plane. I should have *demanded* a C.T. scan. My father would have done as much, and so much more, for me.

But I didn't. I didn't realize the seriousness of the situation in time and, as a result of my blindness, my father is dead.

I had shed no tear since that day five months ago, because to do so would be to rip myself apart, to break the dam that holds me together.

But there on the dusty floor of the Notre Dame Cathedral, at last I spilled my pain. I wept for the man who fed me with a baby spoon and changed my diapers, even as I poisoned myself with the knowledge of all I had not done for him. My only consolation was that I loved him. This he knew for certain, and if he could have seen my tears today, they would have saddened him.

I walked on, farther and farther away from the truth, orbiting my pain. I moved northward, stopped for a moment at the corner of Richlieu and Saint Marc to drink a coffee; but I knew it was time to make for home. I bottled my father up inside me once and for all, swallowed the amulet, and stepped into the cold.

Another Confession
January 12, 2005

Here is another confession: I am tired of speaking French. I am tired of ordering lunch while wondering what the waiter might bring. I am ready to order a medium coffee and actually get it.

The yoga classes have been interesting in this regard. They have been a veritable anatomy lesson in French. I have learned to recognize French words for hips, knees, feet, ankles and toes. But if I hear *tirez* (the French word for pull), one more time, I may, and probably will, scream.

Yes, I look forward to ordering a pint of lager, using just those words, and a handful of chips; London, my friends, will let me do just that, and London is where I will go tomorrow.

Reflection
January 13, 2005

My final day in Paris was an icy, sunny one. Massive exercise on each of the preceding three days had finally worn me out, so I decided to skip yoga altogether and make directly for the Champs Elysees. This, in and of itself, would be a walk of many miles, and one that needed to be completed before noon—for I had a return date with the Eurostar bound for London.

I moved west via Haussmann, taking in the cafés and bakeries that epitomize Paris. I got lost somewhere near Havre-Caumartin, pulling up for a map check at a sunny little café at the corner of Malesherbes and D'Anjou. As fate would have it, I was right where I needed to be, in every sense of the word: on the map, in my heart, in my life. I was infused again with gratitude.

It is not enough to simply write, or paint or compose, I reflected; *authenticity* is the one true art, and life itself the only meaningful *oeuvre*. I wrote a poem for my future wife, Grace:

> *Climb with me*
> *For the higher ground;*
> *My hand is strong—take it.*
> *My word is my will.*
> *I shall not break it.*

I walked on, completing the long, cold

circuit of the day, then made at once for London.

The River Flows
January 13, 2005

The Eurostar slithered away into industrial Paris, a glimpse of Sacré Coeur melting into the distance with a pale sun behind. A mirror of light raced along the empty tracks beside me, keeping pace. From the undercarriage came the quintessential sounds of a train: rhythmic chatter, deeper, random noises, unexpected squeals. It was palpable at last: I was going home.

There have been few times in my life when I felt as I did now, eyes red with exhaustion, yet heart soaring for joy; it was another of those dualities, and yet a contradiction that made sense to me. The voyage had both stripped me to the barest vessel of a self and filled me to the brim. There was nothing at all odd about putting it that way.

Buildings disappeared and minutes swallowed

even their memories; sheep flew by at one hundred miles an hour, never looking up at the train. It was the French countryside in winter: brown furrows, flat green fields, Van Gogh cypress trees; cold-looking lakes and naked deciduous forests. A hard blue sky turned out in clouds of Grecian marble.

You might say this was but a fantasy, a kind of metaphoric dream; but so is all of life, flying past without regard for the train. Is it indeed the train, or the landscape that is moving? And are those sheep, those trees without leaves, solutions to the problem of life, or merely manifestations of its mad design?

Here I cast before your eyes a blue-gray river, and place upon its barely moving waters a small boat possessed of groaning oarlocks and a tired old man. What does it mean? For me the river flows away to nowhere, and the village that flies past is but a galaxy of dreams, worldviews, longings. Candles burned against the blazing of the sun in mortal envy of its timeless flames.

But never mind the light of the sun. Nothing, *nothing* I tell you, is timeless; the sun expires, and all is fantasy.

Yeah, never mind. The train has nosed into the tunnel, and once again I am beneath the sea.

London

London, Once More
January 13, 2005

I emerged into a sunset over England, and spied something I had been longing to see for more than a month: the winsome crescent of a new moon. This was the ultimate marker of the passage of time, the proclamation of my return. It had been long enough, and I was glad to see it. Suddenly the sun vanished; in the darkened sky the wisp of moon pulsed with a light become more fervent, pointing the way home.

Wormhole
January 14, 2005

It is not yet dawn on the final day of my

wandering, but I have been up for hours, excitement coursing through me like electric shocks. And now, with the streets of London still as dark as the boatman's forearms, I am exactly where you would expect to find me: sitting alone at the Café Nero, writing.

It is time to give thanks, to take a kind of final accounting. If I were a cat, bringing to porch the gophers of my voyage, they would be these:

I have traveled nearly fourteen thousand miles, walked three continents, spent thirty-three nights in foreign beds, in London, Paris, Delhi, Agra, Jaipur, Calcutta, Bangalore and Cochin. I have traveled by bus, ferry, taxi, train, rickshaw, rowboat and elephant, and spent more than fifty-four hours in the air. I have endured, and recovered from, two serious illnesses, and walked well in excess of two hundred and fifty miles.

I have been to India's north, middle and southern tip, have been seen by hundreds of thousands, if not millions, of eyes, and touched by as many hands. And I have come to know the people of India, the kindest folk I have ever had the pleasure to encounter.

I have been to Mahatma Gandhi's tomb, walked the slums of Calcutta, and seen the wonder of Mother Teresa's nuns. I have smelled more garbage, urine and feces, and seen more dead bodies, than in all my life—or, I daresay, twenty lives. I survived a solo trek up Otub Road.

I walked alone on windswept, desolate islands, crossed broad straits in little dinghies, heaved the Chinese fishing nets. I was witness to the odd, persistent energy of Yogananda. I met my boatman and heard his strangely moving tale. And I practiced yoga in the Taj Mahal on Christmas day.

I have written two hundred pages, and have taken one thousand seven hundred and eighty-four photographs, a body of work in celebration of the poetry of the moment, the little miracles that surround us every day, just waiting to be observed.

And in the end, I have started to come to terms with my father's death.

It is time to go home.

Soon, I will stand at the place in the center of Piccadilly Circus where I first popped up into this distant world so many weeks ago. And instantly it will happen: I will be sucked into the London Underground as by a child slurping on a straw, into a kind of wormhole that will take me all the way home.

When next I set foot on Mother Earth, I will be on the other side of the planet, having achieved re-entry, walking in unfamiliar shoes that are my own.

Postscript
CalcuttaFund.org

Upon his return from India, Joseph Anderson founded the Calcutta Children's Permanent Fund, an endowment providing medical and nutritional support to the street children of Calcutta.

His photographs of India are on traveling exhibition. They can also be viewed online at www.CaluttaFund.org.

Acknowledgements

I am deeply indebted to the people who made this little volume possible: to Kevin Watson, for believing in the book enough to publish it, to Elisa Barger for her handsome cover design, and especially to Linda Landau, for patiently typing the manuscript. Without you, this book would not be.

I also thank my mother for urging me to take this journey in the wake of my father's unexpected death—and my wife Grace for allowing me to return home after being away for so long! And I honor the memory of my father, without whose wisdom and perspective I could never have embraced what I learned in India.

— Joseph

JOSEPH ANDERSON was born and raised on the California Central Coast. He was educated at the University of California at Berkley, where he received degrees in philosophy and English. He went on to earn his Juris Doctor from Harvard Law School in 1989 and is now a board certified trial lawyer representing victims of nursing home abuse, medical negligence, and aviation disasters. He is also a licensed pilot.

Joseph and his wife Grace, a concert cellist, recently celebrated the birth of their first child, a daughter they named Georgia.

Cover Designer

ELISA BARGER says, "My life has been inspired by a grand passion for the arts. I've always had a love for drawing, painting and music."

During her twenty-year career, Elisa has worked for a nationally known magazine publisher, an advertising and marketing agency, a newspaper and a printing company. She has designed a variety of media including packaging for Planters Lifesavers, logos for Pepsi Direct and promotional material for Wachovia and Wake Forest University. She has also designed CD covers and promotional materials for nationally known musicians. She majored in Commercial (Graphic) Design and minored in Business at Appalachian State University and Peace College. Elisa is now self-employed as ElisaDesigns (www.elisadesigns.com).

"Love is not something we find 'out there' in the world; it is a capacity we discover within ourselves."

—Joseph Anderson

Calcutta Children's Permanent Fund

The purpose of this fund is to establish a permanent endowment of overhead-free funding to organizations providing direct medical and nutritional services to Calcutta's poorest children. The fund is unique in applying the concept of a permanent endowment, which can never be depleted, to the problems of street children in Calcutta's slums. The fund takes advantage of modern investment strategies to achieve leverage for the benefit of those children. All donations are tax-deductible and are added directly to the permanent fund, the corpus of which will never be spent. The annual earnings from the fund's investments go solely to the support of the health and welfare of the children of Calcutta, in perpetuity. The Community Foundation of Greater Greensboro manages the fund. All overhead expenses are paid by Joseph and Grace Anderson.

www.CalcuttaFund.org

The Light Within: A Travel Log of India

Book Club Discussion Guide

1. What, if anything, do you know about the practice of yoga? Who is Bikram Choudhury? Why is the author going to India?

2. India is a place of extremes, juxtaposition, and dichotomy. Can you think of examples from the book where one thing is shown in stark contrast to another?

3. Pollution is described in vivid detail. How does it affect the people who live in it?

4. Why does the author "harden his eyes" when he first encounters the people of India? Does his attitude change by the end of his journey? If so, why?

5. How does the author respond to beggars he meets? What is the reason for his actions?

6. When the author encounters a street

performer, who cruelly controls a bear by a chain he has fastened through the animal's nose, why does the author say, "The whole affair sickened me. So, like a good tourist, I photographed it"? What is the author suggesting about the role of visitors to this place? Is voyeurism to blame for the bear's situation?

7. In "Tidal Wave," which school of thought do you most identify with: Nietzsche's idea of the "eternal recurrence of the same" or the idea of "a source, a fountainhead, an exploding Prime Mover"? Which one best describes the author's mindset?

8. Discuss the irony the author encounters at the gem purveyor's shop in Jaipur. Why is the author disappointed with the children after he gives them a bag of dried potatoes? What can you infer from the outcome of his actions? Is the situation futile?

9. Why, after having refused beggars for days in India, does the author finally relent when he comes upon the beggar in New Market?

10. Why does the author celebrate the New Year with a feast when there are "corpses

burning at Tamil Nadu…and more than one hundred thousand souls drowned in the Indian Ocean and Arabian Sea"? Why does the author suggest that "We must celebrate what is, as it is, while it is"?

11. In the face of our own mortality, what does the author suggest is the only thing worth aspiring to?

12. Why is the author shocked when he returns to the airport in Delhi? What has happened to make him see it in such a different way?

13. When the author returns to Paris, how has he changed? How are the streets of Paris described in contrast to those he saw in India? What does the author suggest that India has amid its filth and chaos that Paris and the rest of the western world does not?

14. What is the mission of CalcuttaFund.org? What can you do to help make a difference?

Joseph Anderson will gladly meet with your book club by phone, online chat or in person at no cost. To reserve a time for your book club, contact Press 53 at editor@press53.com.

.